Professor A. C. Cheyne
An Appreciation

by Richard A. Riesen

SCOTTISH CHURCH HISTORY SOCIETY
EDINBURGH

SCOTTISH CHURCH HISTORY SOCIETY

EDITOR

Professor James Kirk, M.A. Ph.D., D.Litt., F.R.Hist.S, F.R.S.E.
Honorary Professorial Research Fellow in Ecclesiastical History
School of Divinity
University of Glasgow G12 8QQ

© Scottish Church History Society 2006

All communications should be addressed to:
Rev. William D. Graham, M.A. B.D.
Honorary Secretary
48 Corbiehill Crescent, Edinburgh, EH4 5BD

First published 2006

Typeset by Nancy R McGuire, Aberdeenshire

Printed and bound by
Cromwell Press, Trowbridge, Wilts.

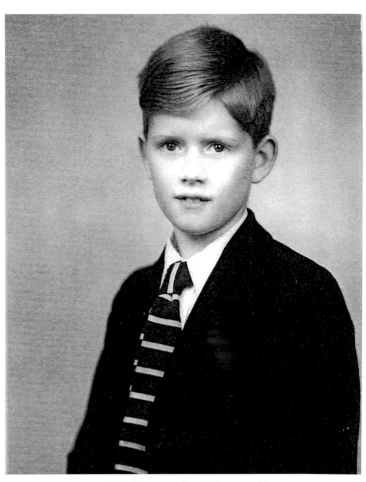

A. C. Cheyne, about 11 years old
Probably Kirkcaldy, c.1935

TABLE OF CONTENTS

ACKNOWLEDGEMENTS

Many thanks to Professor James Kirk and the Scottish Church History Society for the opportunity to publish. My debt to Professor D. W. D. Shaw for his appreciation of Professor Cheyne in the *Festschrift* of 2000 is obvious throughout what I have written here. Kind language is also due to Professor Stewart J. Brown for his generous help with the section on Liberal Historiography and, no less, to Professor David F. Wright, who took the labouring oar on the bibliography of Professor Cheyne's work. Thanks also to Professor Brown and the Reverend Jack Kellet for permission to use their remarks made at the funeral in Stobo. These were all friends and colleagues of Professor Cheyne, perhaps especially Professor Shaw. It is a double pleasure therefore to acknowledge their contributions.

~

1
Introduction

~

THE idea for an appreciation of Professor Cheyne came several years ago as I was reading up for a little primer I was writing on Christian education. In the course of doing so I had occasion to look again at the fine essays by Herbert Butterfield on 'Christianity and History', as well as his more famous book by the same title. The essays were edited and the introduction written by C. T. McIntyre and included a helpful biographical sketch of Butterfield, a pleasant if not necessary companion to the historian's thought. Who, after all, is not interested in the man or woman behind the writing?

As I read McIntyre on Butterfield I wondered, has anyone thought of doing a similar thing for Professor Cheyne? My own debt to him was great, as was that of plenty of others. Was it not time therefore that someone produced something along this line for him?

When I wrote to Professor Cheyne with what I had in mind, he responded with characteristic modesty, even a certain embarrassment—and informed me that a *festschrift* in his honor was in fact on the way and would include an appreciation. He would see that I got one.

Shortly I did get one. Edited by Stewart J. Brown and George Newlands (T&T Clark, 2000), *Scottish Christianity in the Modern World* was a selection of essays organized into two sections: 'Faith and Doubt' and 'Church, State and Society', all the essays having to do with the Church of Scotland from the eighteenth century to the present, a field of study, as the editors point out, in which Professor Cheyne made pioneering contributions. And it did indeed include an appreciation, a sensitive piece by Professor Cheyne's long-time friend Professor D. W. D. Shaw.

Why then anything more? I suppose it was my own very personal interest in Professor Cheyne's life and thought, inspired by my thankfulness for his many kindnesses, and not inconsiderable influence, that prompted this somewhat expanded study: 'somewhat expanded' because it is in fact Professor Shaw's general outline of 'teacher, scholar, churchman, man of culture— and friend' that serves as the basis for what I offer here, and to him I gladly acknowledge my debt.

The project began in earnest with a visit to Peebles in April of 2002, tape recorder in hand, to get down answers to questions prepared in advance. Over dinner at restaurants in Edinburgh and Peebles, over (plenty of!) tea and biscuits in the Crossland Crescent sitting room, on walks to and from bus or meals, we talked—my wife and I and Professor Cheyne—about the subjects outlined, or just as often about anything that took our fancy. Apart from the considerable use the conversations would be as material for a manuscript, they were delightful in and of themselves—lots of wisdom, lots of laughter, lots to remember with fondness. Especially charming was Professor Cheyne himself: relaxed and candid, never anything but charitable and gracious, to be sure, but at his best when airing an opinion. He was through and through an academic, widely read, with a remarkable memory, perhaps especially for verse; but he was also very funny, his humour sharpest when expressing preferences or prejudices, as when he described rock music (he could not remember exactly what it was called!) as 'that awful insistent thump music'. Or his answer to the question whether he had read much of Hemingway: 'Oh, no, I'm sorry'—sides of the man you would probably never see in the classroom. And rightly so, because he knew his job there was to teach, and he had too keen a sense of responsibility not to stick to his last, not to do it very well indeed, not to allow himself to be side-tracked—although, as his students learned to appreciate, his humour was never absent there either. He could bring the house down with his wit, as Professor Shaw reminds us.

Further trips to Peebles (in 2004 and 2005) and further correspondence followed in an attempt to get it right, and to get Professor Cheyne's benediction. There were letters, too, to his friends and former pupils to solicit tributes or reminiscences. A modest portrayal, not a full-fledged biography, is what I hoped to achieve.

To Professor Shaw's 'teacher, scholar, churchman, man of culture—and friend' I have presumed therefore to add 'early life', 'student', 'soldier', 'divinity student' and 'professor'. There are, as well, Professor Cheyne's reflections on his experience at Oxford and on the men and women who influenced him most, plus something on the shape of his intellectual and religious convictions: his rootedness in 'the tradition of liberal historiography' referred to by Professors Brown and Newlands, and the Liberal Evangelicalism mentioned by Professor Shaw— both of special interest to me and both of course indispensable to an appreciation of the man either as man or as scholar and teacher. My brief comments in 'In Mufti' are an attempt to say something about him 'out of uniform', on his less professional and more personal side. The penultimate section is a brief look at two lectures Professor Cheyne considered, significantly, his best work; the conclusion takes up what is perhaps the real theme of these remarks, the relationship of piety and learning.

This should not be taken, though, as in any sense an 'intimate portrait'—no probing or unseemly familiarity. All such would be entirely inappropriate to the man. Nor is it a dissertation, as neither of us would have cared to worry over another of those! It is simply an appreciation, born of affection, respect and gratitude.

Many would agree that a very great deal of Professor Cheyne's effectiveness, not to say attractiveness, was attributable to the combination in him of a genuine Christian faith and a broad catholicity, a kind of saneness or temperateness—not diffidence, to be sure (he had definite and well-considered views on most things!), but a tolerance that invited rather than discouraged inquiry as well as trust. Thus was he the perfect graduate adviser, the role in which his admirers remember him most. He seemed able somehow to provide direction that was at the same time both firm and gentle, decided but not dogmatic. It is that generous spirit that I hope comes across in the sketches that follow. If it does I shall have done my job. I can only hope that he might have thought so too.

~

2

Home and Early Years

~

ALEXANDER Campbell Cheyne was born on 1 June 1924 in Errol, Perthshire, son of the Reverend Alexander Cheyne, United Free Church Minister of Errol, and Catherine Anna Campbell.

Alec's mother's father, Alexander Campbell (after whom A. C. was named), was an architectural draughtsman; 'i.e., a dogsbody to an architect who got most of the credit—and money'. There is still a big hotel in Strathpeffer, near Inverness, that was designed by him. But he was never well off, and the home in which the Campbells lived after their return to the north from Paisley was owned by Alec's grandmother's brother, John Young, who became a well-known draper in Inverness. 'My great-grandmother [Alec's mother's mother] was, I suspect, illiterate: she was certainly Gaelic-speaking'.

Alec's mother was brought up in Inverness and educated at Inverness Royal Academy (a non-fee-paying school). 'I believe she was a good student; she was certainly medalist in French'. She had four siblings: Jack (who later taught New Testament at Wooster in Ohio, at Yale, and—after a time as parish minister at Kilmacolm, near Glasgow—at Westminster College, Cambridge); Alexander Elmslie (the top medical graduate of his year at Aberdeen, who saw military service chiefly in Greece and practised medicine in Surrey after the First World War); Margaret (graduated in French and Latin at Aberdeen; taught in Auchterarder and subsequently in an Anglican sisterhood near London); and Dorothy, 'the un-academic one', who spent her entire working life in a bank in Inverness.

The Campbell family had many 'religious connections'. In addition to Alec's mother's brother Jack, mentioned above (a New College graduate and an exact contemporary of Donald Baillie), who ministered in Peterculter before going to teach in the United States, there was his mother's father, a 'session clerk' and respected elder of the Crown Church, Inverness, and his mother's uncle, John Young, who married a daughter of John Mackay, a celebrated Highland minister.

There were religious connections on Alec's father's side as well. 'My father's mother's family, the Riddels, also had some notable characters', he said. William Riddel, for example, Alec's granny's eldest brother, who graduated in Arts and Medicine and Theology at Aberdeen, spent the greater part of his life as a medical missionary with the English Presbyterian Church in central China. There was also Alec Riddel, one of William's brothers, who went out to Africa in 1875 as an agricultural missionary with the expedition, led by Dr Robert Law, which founded Livingstonia as a memorial to the great missionary-explorer.

It is not surprising therefore that it was under 'religious circumstances' that father and mother met— while Catherine was housekeeper in Jack's manse in Peterculter in Aberdeenshire and Alexander was minister in neighbouring Maryculter. They married in 1923 and in 1924 moved south to Errol, between Perth and Dundee, a lovely fruit-growing part of Scotland. A year after Alec, a sister, Mona, was born, in 1925, and a brother, George, in 1927.

Father had trained in Classics and Divinity at Aberdeen and Glasgow, and served in the Great War (1914–18) as an officer in the Gordon Highlanders. His great experience was at the Somme in 1916. Though not a disciplinarian in the home, nor apparently among his troops, he was nonetheless 'in battle a lion', according to a testimonial written by one of his superior officers. A small-farmer's son from Buchan, Aberdeenshire, he was much closer to the ordinary soldier than officers trained from the gentry—one of the reasons for the superior effectiveness of Scots officers with their men in combat. He was an infantry officer, a platoon commander, and was wounded in the final German attack in 1918. He survived only by commandeering a wheelbarrow and ordering an enlisted man to push him in it to safety! After the war he returned to finish his studies in divinity, but not at Aberdeen, as it held too many memories of friends lost in the fighting. He went rather to Glasgow where he took his B.D. in (it seems)1920.

From his pastorate in Errol he moved his family in 1928 to Kirkcaldy, Fife, where he would serve as minister of Dunnikier United Free Church, which was to become, a year later (with the union of 1929), Dunnikier Church of Scotland. Alec recalled his mother's description of how her heart sank as they drove into Kirkcaldy: 'it was just factories', she said.

Life in the Cheyne household was pleasant, 'very gentle', Alec remembered, as neither parent was terribly strict. It was 'not a harsh regime at all', although 'there were certain boundaries you didn't cross. You didn't talk back, for one'. For instance, 'I never felt I was being compelled to go to church', Alec said, 'although I don't know what would've been done if you said you were *not* going—because we never tried it'.

Besides a gentle home, it was, within financial limits, a cultured home. Father was a good violinist, 'a fiddler, as he called himself'. Mona was an exceptional musician and George 'almost as good'. Both parents were fond of music and wanted the children to be fond of it too.

There was also plenty of literary talk. When mother and father were 'just getting to know one another', father once quoted a line from Shakespeare's *Winter's Tale* ('daffodils, that come before the swallow dares'), and mother promptly finished it ('And take the winds of March with beauty'). Mother knew 'a great deal more than father' about literature, though. She was an enthusiastic Dickens fan, and kept up with reading, 'Yeats and Company, for instance'. This indeed was a matrimonial match—and the foundation for the blessedly cultured mansc that shaped the tastes and character of Alexander, Mona, and George.

~

3

Student

~

IT was in Kirkcaldy in 1930, then, that the eldest son, Alexander Campbell, entered Kirkcaldy High Primary School (the primary school was attached to the high school) and later, in 1936, Kirkcaldy High School.

It should be noted that the schools young Cheyne attended were public schools, in large part because his parents believed in state-run education. In fact, during his time at Kirkcaldy Primary School, when it was decided that the school should be fee-paying (it was not a large fee), his parents were mightily perturbed, not because of the cost but because of the principle. Here was set, too, the temper of Alec's political persuasion.

At Kirkcaldy High School Alec was a diligent student, ending his studies as *Dux*, although that was 'not so astonishing', he said, because 'competition was hardly great in a class of about thirty'. It was nonetheless promise early on of the academic distinction that would follow.

From Kirkcaldy Alec matriculated at the University of Edinburgh, thinking he would do English (the literary influences in his home?), but his approach to the subject and the department's were different, he said, although he didn't say in what respect. So he decided for History, thanks partly to the inspiration of a fine teacher at school, and above all, to the brilliant lectures of the great medievalist, Professor V. H. Galbraith, in the university. It was a decision to be vindicated by his success, both future and immediate. He graduated with First Class Honours in 1946, winning the Kirkpatrick Prize as the top student in History that year.

Was there ever any question about where Alec would attend university? His father dismissed St Andrews somewhat derisively, and Oxford was out because it was wartime and the less travelling one did the better ('I don't think Oxford was even considered in 1942'). So the choice was Edinburgh, and for the first three years Alec travelled by train to and from Kirkcaldy, 'with blackout lights, over-crowded compartments, and so on'. The train took about an hour, but with interruptions (and when there was light enough) he could count on about forty-five minutes each way for reading.

~

4
Soldier

~

A LEC'S university years (1942–46) coincided almost exactly with those of the war. 'I expected to be called up the end of my first year in the university', he recalled, but for some reason was not. He did, though, serve in the Home Guard Corps of Signals during those years, as did his father. His call-up came finally in his fourth year, but when he reported to Dr David Horn, who was in charge of the history department's 'administrative side of things', that he might have to go into the Army, Dr Horn said, 'Well, we must raise Heaven and earth to stop this!' He then went 'right to the phone' and got a six month's extension, which of course 'made all the difference'.

Alec's original registration was with the Royal Scots, but after graduation he was sent first for general training to Lichfield and then to Redford Barracks in Colinton, outside of Edinburgh, for training with the Black Watch. 'I thought I'd been sent to Hell', was the way he put it.

After basic training Alec went immediately to the Army School of Education at Alton Towers, Staffordshire, and soon became an instructor there, teaching potential sergeants (those who manned the education corps), but 'nothing even remotely military'. His job was rather to assess their teaching ability, to critique their performance, also to give occasional lectures on history to larger audiences fresh out of university. (Once when he was lecturing on the Elizabethan period a troop of 'brass hats' came in, 'colonels and so on', and it was 'kind of scary, really!')

With his university education, Alec of course could have been an officer, but he did not want to be, he said, 'not from any high principles', rather because he had no desire to go through the training, which was 'quite fearsome'. He did, however, get himself promoted to Warrant Officer 2, then Warrant Officer 1, the highest rank available to him. 'There was tremendous amusement amongst all my friends and acquaintances', he recalled, over his having attained this rather exalted position, because he was supposed to be 'mildly military' to do so, which, he admitted, he certainly was not. Once, when he had to order his platoon to march in a parade, for instance, they all 'just rocked with laughter'. 'Oh, please do this properly', he said, 'We're on a parade'. National service was hardly Alec's cup of tea!

Even as a soldier, though, he acquitted himself admirably. A testimonial written on 9 June 1948, on his release from national service, described his military conduct as 'very good', and went on to say that he was 'a first-class warrant officer – an excellent instructor of high grade intelligence – he is diligent and accurate in his work – takes great pains and is thoroughly conscientious, sober and honest, he is self-reliant, loyal and full of enterprise. He has an excellent sense of humour – is correct in attitude both to Juniors as well as Seniors – can and does accept responsibility and is very loyal. He has a most engaging personality and is well liked by his fellow men. Will certainly do well in whatever sphere he is employed'. Nor were the two years without their satisfactions. 'I enjoyed a lot of it very much', he said, and, as the Second World War had ended and the Korean War had not yet begun, 'I was mighty lucky'.

~

5
Oxford

~

IF military life was not exactly Alec's cup of tea, Oxford was. Following his two years of national service he went to Oriel ('Newman's College') for another two years, the idea having been suggested by friends in the Army, and the experience turned out to be 'just delightful'. What made the stint at Oxford possible was a Carnegie Scholarship of £250, enough to live on in those days. In addition he was fortunate enough to obtain a Cross Scholarship (named after Sir Alexander Cross, a scion of the Coats family who had made its fortune in cotton manufacturing) of £175.

The idea of the Cross Scholarship was that you went to Oxford not just to study, but 'to get the whole cultural life of Oxford, and you needed money for that'. In preparation Alec went to Sir Alexander's estate in Battleby, Perthshire with several other Scots lads (the Cross Scholarship was given only to Scots) to be instructed by Cross on 'how to behave' in Oxford, 'how to lay a table and so on'. As Cross had been to Oxford himself, he greatly esteemed the type of education provided there, and 'wanted us to fit into the Oxford scene'. 'I thought it was a good idea', Alec reflected.

The difference between going up to Oxford and going up to Edinburgh was tremendous, he recalled. Later, in writing reminiscences of student life at Edinburgh and Oriel, Alec reckoned that a comparison of the reception he got at Oriel and the one he got at Edinburgh 'did not favour Edinburgh'. For one thing, the appearance of class distinction was, ironically, greater at Edinburgh than at Oxford. The day he showed up to register at Edinburgh in the Old College, for instance, he remembered that there were 'rows of Edinburgh schoolboys, Watsonians and Herioters, and so on, looking down on us humble folk from Kirkcaldy and places like that'.

Making matters worse, the staff in the matriculation office at Edinburgh were 'so unpleasant'. By contrast, 'about three weeks before I went up to Oxford, I got a letter from the lodgings, saying, "Sorry, we can't take you after all." (I think they'd been offered more money or something.) I didn't know what to do'. Alec's mother advised that he write a letter to the Dean of Oriel 'telling him you're in a fix'. He did, and back came a reply informing him that he had rooms at the college for a year, which were renewed for a second year. 'And that's the difference' between Edinburgh and Oxford, said Alec. Oxford was, 'if anything, more democratic'.

The result of Alec's work at Oriel was a B.Litt., 'a kind of mini-Ph.D.' (the degree is no longer offered). The thesis was 'Anglo-Scottish Relations under William and Mary and Anne, 1688–1714', for which he had to read, mostly, the Sharp Manuscripts held by the Archbishop of York, as well as the Argyll Papers. It was, in other words, a research degree, but 'a kind of apprentice one'. Still, as Alec said, it was 'quite a substantial thing—I've got it bound—but I've never done anything with it'. He didn't finish the degree, in fact, until he was a student at New College; and although he worked 'quite hard' at Oxford, it wasn't 'a whole-time job'.

While at Oxford Alec attended meetings of the now-famous Socratic Club, presided over by C. S. Lewis as a forum where Christians could dispute their beliefs with unbelievers. He was also present at Pusey House when T. S. Eliot delivered his lecture on The New English Bible ('Eliot wasn't much impressed with it') and a member of the Christian Socialist Club—'never had any inclination to vote Conservative my whole life', he said.

~

6

Lecturer

~

FOLLOWING Oxford, 'I didn't know what I was going to do. I always had in the back of my mind the ministry, but I didn't know quite what kind of ministry I was going to conduct'. In his indecision Alec's father sent him two cuttings from the newspaper, one advertising a lectureship at King's College, London, and one a lectureship at the University of Glasgow. He applied for both and was summoned for interview at both, but Glasgow appointed him before he had a chance to go to London. In his favour in getting the Glasgow appointment was that the Professor of History at Glasgow, Andrew Browning, 'a very distinguished historian', had been his external examiner for his first degree at Edinburgh. Crowning the appointment was a note from Oriel College dated only 19 June (1950 no doubt) from Vivian Galbraith. It says simply: 'I am quite delighted and congratulate you …. You will find in Browning the best of chiefs. Let me know how you get on'. There follows a lovely postscript: 'And if you ever call me "Sir" again, I'll … well, I shall be disappointed'.

Alec's tenure at Glasgow (1950–53) was 'a very good three years'. The first year he did nothing but mark papers and conduct tutorials, but at the end he was appointed lecturer, a post he held for his remaining time there. On his appointment as lecturer, Professor Browning told him he was to take the second-year class for historians and English specialists, 'The Age of Chaucer to the Age of Shakespeare (1307–1625)'. This was 'of course almost the only period I had never studied seriously before'. That first year lecturing was therefore (as every first-year teacher must know) 'a hand to mouth existence. You had to give about seventy-five lectures in a period of about six months'. Lectures at Glasgow then were fifty minutes each. They were also, according to Alec, fun, although the young lecturer was not always sure what to do about student discipline, 'dealing with smart-alecs and jokers in the class'. The third year Professor Browning asked him to take the Honours Class on the Tudor period. In those days 'lecturing' meant that one had a period of history and could organize it any way he liked ('back to front if I'd wanted to'), although the Honours Class was more a seminar, 'sitting round a table'.

Glasgow was 'a great city and a lovely university' and 'just slightly more democratic than Edinburgh'. The students came, some of them, from quite poor backgrounds, and a great many, being Irish, were Catholics. 'There were umpteen Maria Theresas and Francis Xaviers', Alec recalled, and his closest friend on the staff was the Catholic historian Dr J. J. Tumelty, a great influence on him.

7

Divinity Student

PERHAPS of most significance for Alec's future, and that of his students, was that already at Glasgow, and especially in teaching the Tudor period, he was 'getting hooked on the ecclesiastical'. While at Glasgow, in fact, Alec decided to go into the ministry, a matter over which 'I'd been agonizing for years'. The thing that had been keeping him back was the question, 'How does one do the job in an effective way?' The solution came in his association with Tom Allan's congregation in North Kelvinside. Allan was later one of those responsible for bringing Billy Graham to Scotland and 'a wonderful man'; and although Alec's association with Allan was in Allan's 'pre-Billy Graham phase', Alec thought that in what he saw in North Kelvinside, 'Tom Allan had the answer'.

Allan was an Evangelical, but 'an intellectual Evangelical, and very strong on parish visitation and things like that'. There were weekly meetings on a Wednesday evening where there was 'a certain amount of biblical exposition', and then Allan would 'just sort of talk to us about anything he thought might be interesting and useful. I got caught up in the visitation thing and went round some very slummy places in Glasgow', Alec remembered. All this was drawing him into the parish ministry.

But of course there was his father's example as well: 'He was a pastor and I thought he'd done a pretty good job'. In addition there was, interestingly, his teaching at Glasgow. There, 'I suddenly realized that I had a kind of pastoral view of students and I found that I was wanting more for them than I could provide as a lecturer. That definitely was a consideration'.

Was it not, though, primarily a spiritual thing, a calling? Well, yes, but 'there was no kind of blinding light or anything. It was all quite difficult working it out'. So in an exercise of the sort of wisdom and humility one might expect of young Alec Cheyne, he scheduled an interview to discuss his dilemma with John Baillie, then Professor of Divinity at New College and a kind of hero, as well as a friend of the family on his mother's side. At the end of the interview Professor Baillie told him two things: first, if you're having this much difficulty making your mind up, then whichever way you go it'll be all right; and second, when you've made the decision you'll realize that this was what was going to happen all the time. As Alec left, Professor Baillie said, 'If you do decide to come to New College, then we'll all throw our hats into the air'. Baillie was 'a great man', Alec reflected, and his brother Donald 'a saintly kind of man'.

After Professor Baillie's encouragement, it is difficult to imagine what other choice Alec could have made.

Indeed he did decide for New College and the ministry, and in 1956 graduated B.D. (Distinction in Ecclesiastical History), with no thought of ever teaching again. 'In fact I thought it would be a bit grotesque if I gave up lecturing and then went back to it'.

At one point, however, he seriously considered going abroad to teach in a mission college in India, which would not have required ordination. But while Alec was in conversation about this with the overseas missions secretary of the Church of Scotland in the hallway at New College, Professor J. H. S. Burleigh, Professor of Ecclesiastical History, passed by and said to the secretary, 'Leave that man alone; he's coming to succeed me'. 'Of course I didn't really believe it at that stage', he said—as inevitable as it all might seem in hindsight. Another change in direction, back this time to teaching, was in the offing.

The right people, and the best people, were, for a start, on Alec's side. The famous John Baillie was a friend of the family, and Burleigh knew his background in history. Moreover, 'there hadn't been all that many firsts in history who'd gone into the ministry'. It was the combination then of the first at Edinburgh, the research at Oxford, the teaching in the Army, and especially at Glasgow, that distinguished him, not to mention his excellent references and the fact that 'I was doing okay in theology—no problem', he said. The invitation also came 'at just the right time'.

Thus would the future Professor of Ecclesiastical History be launched on his teaching career. But not for almost another two years. In 1956, following his graduation from New College, Alec was granted (with an Aitken Fellowship from Edinburgh) a post-graduate year on the continent, first at Tübingen to study German, then at Basel to study theology under Karl Barth and Oscar Cullman, among others.

He returned to Edinburgh in July of 1957, but from then until February 1958 he travelled around Scotland as a 'probationer', filling preaching vacancies. He was going 'all over the place', applying to some of the churches he had visited but 'getting nowhere'. (He tells of going to Oban where, when he got up to read the lesson, he opened a Gaelic Bible which, of course, he could not read). His not being married was also something of a problem.

~

8
Professor

~

JUST when it looked as if a country church in Midlothian might be interested in him, Professor Burleigh asked him to come to New College. 'James McEwen is going to Aberdeen', Burleigh said, 'and I'd like you to succeed him'. Still thinking, apparently, that it would be the parish ministry for him, he 'agonized for a day or two'. But in the end, 'I felt, well, it's a bird in the hand. I'd been looking for over a year. So that's the story', he said of his journey from teaching to ministry and back to teaching.

Professor Burleigh remained at New College for six years after Alec was appointed in April 1958. An 'awfully good head of department', Burleigh had himself been in parish work for ten years before coming to New College. After he retired he moved to Peebles where Alec visited him regularly before moving there himself in 1986.

As Burleigh's replacement in the Chair of Ecclesiastical History in 1964, Professor Cheyne introduced both new courses and new styles of teaching: courses in modern Church history, Pietism, Evangelicalism and Tractarianism, for example, as well as seminars ('attached to a document or something'), not as a replacement for, but in addition to the traditional lecture.

Professor Cheyne's lectures were 'always manuscripts', and always written in pen and ink, although he hoped he got 'less tied to them' as the years went by. 'The most successful lecturers read a full manuscript', he reckoned.

His preparation for teaching early on began with 'lots of reading' on the period, followed by the writing of lectures, 'keeping about one step ahead of the class'— again, a process familiar to all young teachers, ancient and modern.

As for the relationship of teacher to students: it was the Scottish tradition to have 'a kind of pastoral interest' in one's students; indeed in earlier times the teacher was often someone 'who would've liked to be a minister'— thus was the tutor-student relationship at Oxford so appealing to a Scot like Alec. 'The great thing in Oxbridge is your relationship to your tutor', he said. Latterly in Scotland, however, the class had become the lecture, whereas in Oxbridge the lecture was but a report on the lecturer's research, 'class' being the one-on-one with the tutor. By comparison with Oxbridge, then, the Scottish format might be seen as spoon-feeding the student. In any case, the seminar, employed at New College by Professor Cheyne, was an attempt to bridge the gap between the Oxbridge and Edinburgh styles of teaching— and thus perhaps restore to the Scottish system something of its earlier, more intimate character. Nor were there any textbooks as such. 'We'd simply say, "Well, I think you could hardly do better than read

Bainton's *Here I Stand* on Luther", for example, but we wouldn't be examining on Bainton'. Such were some of the changes Professor Cheyne brought to the teaching at New College.

Much of Professor Cheyne's widely-respected effectiveness in teaching, and his enviable popularity, came no doubt from what he described as his family's 'gift of the gab'. All the family, he said, enjoyed speaking informally as well as in public, although not in his own case, he confessed, 'on the spur of the moment'.

What many remember, however, perhaps as much as anything, is how easy it was to take notes in his classes. Even though his lectures had a narrative flow, one could always see the outline; the organization was obvious, and for students that was a boon. Clearly he took his lectures seriously. They were not merely a footnote to his research. They were, as Professor Shaw says, 'meticulously prepared, beautifully structured, and read with energy and enthusiasm'.

With some instructors one had the impression that teaching was a necessary evil—notes cobbled together at the last minute at best, comments off the top of the head at worst; maybe a chapter from their latest book, read without enthusiasm directly from the typescript, interrupted only by their stopping, pen in hand, to amend or emend what had been written and would soon, hopefully, find itself in print. Not so Professor Cheyne. It was clear that his classes were a priority and his lectures a matter of pride. Thorough, carefully organized, obviously well thought out, they were more than merely cogent.

They were interesting. Professor Cheyne had gone out of his way to find a touching, or funny, anecdote to add just the right seasoning. I at least never felt I was being cheated, either because it was all substance and no form—a thorough but uninteresting recitation of fact, perhaps—or an attempt at 'relevance' without serious academic import. With Professor Cheyne you were being taught, with no lack of humour or human interest in the delivery. You got your money's worth. In those days, at Edinburgh, at any rate, lecturing from a manuscript was the accepted procedure. Unacceptable as the practice now is in some quarters, if everyone had been as enjoyable to listen to as Professor Cheyne, there would never have been a problem.

~

9

Scholar

~

THIS emphasis on the quality of Professor Cheyne's teaching puts into context a couple of comments he wanted me especially to hear and went out of his way to make sure I understood. The first had to do with the balance in him between teaching and research, the second with his relationship to other scholars in his own field.

He wanted it understood, first, that he saw himself as a teacher and *not* a researcher. The most protracted research he had done, he reckoned, was for the Oxford degree. Research, he confessed, was 'not really where I feel most at home. Instinctively I am a teacher; I do research when I have to'. From as distinguished a university chair as Professor Cheyne's, and a scholar whose contributions to his field, the editors of the *Festschrift* argue, have been pioneering, this comes as something of a surprise, although not entirely, considering the lament of Professor Shaw, and shared by others, that 'it is future generations' loss that he has not published more'. It also comes as a refreshing, almost disarming, bit of candour, evidence of the man's humility and self-understanding, but further insight, if we needed it, into why he was such a good teacher: he worked hard at his teaching, all right, but teaching was also natural to him.

The second thing he wanted understood was that he realized that he had been more isolated in his work than a more gregarious person might be. He confessed to being naturally shy. 'I would never write to Owen Chadwick about a chapter in a book I was writing, for instance', he said. As a result, 'I have hoed my own furrow', with 'little personal contact about my subject'. What this meant for his scholarship, on reflection, was that 'I could have written better if I'd consulted the living as well as the dead'. On the other hand, it may be that hoeing his own furrow gave to his limited body of research that special quality which rendered it pioneering, uniquely his own in any case.

Whatever the long-term assessment of his academic work, it may be his teaching that will be remembered— revealing, again, the very practical and pastoral side of the man. Professor Cheyne never came across as someone attempting to put his erudition on display. One cannot imagine, for instance, coming away from a Cheyne lecture or conversation thinking, 'Goodness, he is so far above me that I have no idea what he's talking about'. He was a teacher, a communicator, first and last. His teaching was for him an art, perhaps more importantly a ministry. His purpose was not to confuse, or to magnify his reputation as a 'great intellectual'. It was to impart knowledge and understanding—precisely what teachers are supposed to do, and what the best teachers do memorably.

Acknowledgement having been made of Professor Cheyne's preference for teaching over research (and in deference to his wishes it must be made), it would be inaccurate and unjust to leave the matter there. Even a cursory reading of his body of work—a body of work, it should be said, that any of us would be glad to own!—is ample evidence that he was an exceedingly able and thorough researcher and scholar, not to mention a persuasive and engaging writer, ranging in his sources from public documents to private correspondence, from theology to devotion, the arcane or abstract to the particular and the poignantly human. Look at his inaugural lecture on 'Diversity and Development in Scottish Presbyterianism', for example, where we move from the *Scots Confession* to *The Correspondence of the Revd. Robert Wodrow*, from the *Prayer Book of 1637* to *The Whole Proceeding in the Case of John McLeod Campbell before the Presbytery of Dunbarton, and the Synod of Glasgow and Ayr*, from John Tulloch's 'Introductory Lecture delivered at St Mary's College, St Andrews, 21 November, 1864' to A. R. MacEwen's *Life of John Cairns*, to give but a few examples of many—all in support of a closely argued case for the proposition that 'the overall story of Scottish Presbyterianism is one of much controversy and fairly steady change. There has

never been a "golden period" in which 'the full
Presbyterian position' ... is clearly discernible ...'.[1]

Or his essay on 'The Bible and Change in the
Nineteenth Century': from biographies of Thomas
Carlyle and Sir Walter Scott to the theologies of William
Cunningham, R. S. Candlish and the Baptist Robert
Haldane to the Old Testament criticism (and preaching)
of A. B. Davidson, William Robertson Smith and George
Adam Smith, Professor Cheyne unpacks his considered
judgment that 'in all their labours [the biblical critics of
the last half of the nineteenth century] were guided less
by the traditions of the Church and the demands of
dogmatic theology than by what the text actually said to
the well-informed, candid and sensitive mind'.[2]

There is theological depth as well as psychological
insight. Nor are we left without a decision. While
Professor Cheyne was always temperate, modelling his
own conviction that 'with the past in mind, the historian
may well recommend toleration of the differences still
existing and reflect that in a great national Church there
should be room for diversity',[3] he is at the same time
never hesitant to come to a conclusion. We know exactly
where the evidence has led him, as the examples cited,
indeed almost everything he ever wrote, demonstrate.

In what is his only full-length book, and perhaps his
best work, *The Transforming of the Kirk*, Professor
Cheyne provides, for anyone who requires it, more than

[1]   *Studies in Scottish Church History*, p. 31.
[2]   *Ibid.*, p. 131.
[3]   *Ibid.*, p. 12.

sufficient proof of his competence as a scholar/researcher. In a little over 200 pages he charts the revolutionary changes that so shaped the Scottish church in the last half of the nineteenth century, that era, as he puts it, 'which may be said to have begun with Darwin's *Origin of Species* in 1859 and ended with Lloyd George's challenge to the House of Lords at the close of the Edwardian period'[4] and which saw the triumph of a 'fairly cautious liberalism—or open-minded conservatism'[5] over a 'rigid—not to say immobile—orthodoxy'[6] in attitudes toward the Bible, the Westminster Confession of Faith, worship, and the Church's obligation to the poor.

What makes all of this such enjoyable and convincing reading are several things. There is, first, its economy. Not that a good deal more would not be welcome; but the combination of scholarship and brevity gives the work a kind of pace or vitality that draws the reader along, making thoroughly academic employment seem hardly 'academic' at all.

A similar result is achieved by superb organization. There are only five chapters for a start (plus a 'prelude' and a 'postlude'). The structure is simple and clear. From beginning to end we know exactly what the book is about. Although the details might be intimidating, their arrangement renders them entirely manageable. We never lose our way, are never led into a thicket. As in all

---

[4] *Ibid.*, p. 4.
[5] *Ibid.*, p. 218.
[6] *Ibid.*, p. 11.

good writing, especially of this sort, we are kept focused until the point is made, the case closed.

The exercise is not without its amusements, however. There is no lack of human interest, even humour, both of course reinforcing the argument as well as (without ever sacrificing seriousness) making it easy and enjoyable to process. Robert Haldane, for instance, he refers to as 'one never deficient in pugnacity'[7] and William Cunningham as among the 'theological iron-clads'.[8] Of the earlier doctrine of Scripture, he says, 'Scottish believers between 1650 and 1800 were little inclined to question the infallibility of Scripture's pronouncements or even the Almighty's personal responsibility for every syllable contained therein'.[9] One of 'Rabbi' Duncan's lectures on the same subject he labels 'a characteristically idiosyncratic and unclassifiable contribution',[10] and of the worship services at the beginning of the nineteenth century, he remarks: 'The prayers were on occasion barely distinguishable from the sermon, and liable to last almost as long'.[11] There was, too, 'the doctrinaire assumption' of *The Church Hymnary: Third Edition* (this time quoting a letter to *Life and Work*) that 'you make worship Christian if you scatter Trinitarian formulae over it with a pepper-pot'[12]—lending specificity to Professor

---

[7]   *Studies in Scottish Church History*, p. 128.
[8]   *Transforming of the Kirk*, p. 79.
[9]   *Ibid.*, p. 5.
[10] *Ibid.*, p. 7.
[11] *Ibid.*, pp. 17–18.
[12] *Ibid.*, p. 199.

Shaw's perceptive comment regarding Professor Cheyne's success as a lecturer: 'Part of his secret was his eye for the telling quotation'.[13]

As for human interest: so wonderfully peopled are his accounts that it is hard to imagine history from his pen apart from biography, memoir, anecdote, 'telling quotation'. Not even ideas are discussed in the abstract; ideas belong to someone, in a time and place, and that matters. The importance and interest of individuals for him may be reflected in the fact that over half the chapters in *Studies in Scottish Church History* are biographical.

All this contributes to what is perhaps the outstanding characteristic of his writing—its accessibility. He has a remarkable gift for 'translating down'. He writes for the specialist and non-specialist alike. Nowhere is this more evident than in a series of articles he wrote for the Church of Scotland's monthly publication *Life and Work* throughout 1978. Here is the story of the Kirk from John Knox to William Robertson Smith in instalments of a little over two pages apiece, each dealing with what he called 'Turning-Points in Scottish Church History'. Neither unsupported generalization nor incomprehensible detail, the series is simply good history well told, never without evidence of scholarly research, but never out of reach of the interested lay person. Notwithstanding his lasting contribution to the cause of scholarship, it cannot be said of him that he is either too subtle or too

---

[13]   *Scottish Christianity in the Modern World*, p. 11.

complex for the ordinary reader. The same is true of his lectures. That is no doubt why he was both a favourite teacher at graduate level and a much sought-after speaker for audiences as diverse as the St Andrews Summer Institute (noted for its popularity among American pastors) and the Divinity Dames (wonderful name!), a circle for wives of New College students in the days, long ago, before women became the majority there (!).

There is, finally, simply his good writing. Of the influence of German theology on the Scottish churches prior to 1914, for instance, he says: 'Both Cairns of the United Presbyterian Church and Tulloch of the Church of Scotland were much at home in Germany, and a steady stream of theological students followed them until diverted by the Kaiser's War from Berlin, Halle, Marburg and Tübingen to the Marne, Gallipoli and the Somme'.[14] Artfully rendered. Or of the period between the first and second world wars: 'Even from the standpoint of the nineteen seventies and eighties, agonizing and tormented as they are, it looks as if few periods in Scottish history can have been more difficult and discouraging for the Churches than that in which faith reeled from the impact of one great war, nerved itself belatedly for another, and in the interim endured the soul-destroying effects of a seemingly endless economic depression'.[15] These are but samples, representative of what can be found on almost any page of practically everything he wrote. Scholarship—thorough research, thoughtfully analyzed

[14] *Transforming of the Kirk*, p. 72.
[15] *Ibid.*, p. 186.

and organized—is delivered in very enviable prose indeed.

And what does Professor Cheyne's writing tell us about his own views? As it turns out, a good deal. Everywhere one or another of a handful of prominent themes shines through.

First, he clearly took the view that the history of the Church, like all of history, is a thing very various, complicated, not 'smooth-surfaced', as he puts it.[16] The Church is a living, growing, developing organism whose life and thought cannot be captured in a single document or single form, itself the product of a particular time and place. There are of course 'the great essentials', the core, 'concerning which virtual unanimity has almost invariably existed'; but 'with equal truth it may be said that diversity of opinion has always been in evidence'.[17]

But, second, it is not simply the fact of diversity that he wants us to absorb. It is that, given that fact, out of necessity as well as Christian charity and a merely reasonable fair-mindedness, we should learn toleration, moderation, catholicity—the 'lenity and compassion' which he said had characterized the tenure of Robert Rollock, Edinburgh University's first principal.[18]

Nor is it insignificant that 'Diversity and Development in Scottish Presbyterianism' was his inaugural lecture as Professor of Ecclesiastical History in New College. This appreciation for the complexity of events and (especially)

---

[16] *Studies in Scottish Church History,* p. 3.
[17] *Ibid.,* p. 4.
[18] *Ibid.,* p. 38.

of human beings, and therefore the broad-mindedness
required of those who interpret their history, is Professor
Cheyne through and through. Nearly every—it may be
every—churchman he wrote about with admiration—
John Tulloch, John Caird, D. S. Cairns, John and Donald
Baillie—was a man distinguished by his moderation, 'his
eirenic and catholic sympathies', as he says of John
Caird,[19] his 'humility of spirit and receptivity of mind', as
he says of John Tulloch.[20] This essential liberality he
contrasts with whatever seems 'extreme', 'unreasoning',
'dogmatic', 'puritanical', or 'intolerant', either past or
present.

Third, Christian faith was not for Professor Cheyne
primarily a doctrinal or academic thing, and so not tied
to either a 'subordinate standard' or even an inerrant
Bible. The preachers he esteemed—'John Tulloch, John
Caird and Robert Story in the Auld Kirk, and Marcus
Dods, Henry Drummond, Walter C. Smith, and
Alexander Whyte in the Free'—talked, he says, 'more of
love and trust than of intellectual assent, more of religion
than theology'.[21] And because faith is not essentially
propositional, neither is dispute the atmosphere in which
it breathes most freely. Such was his understanding of
authentic belief, and it is a piece with his Liberal
Evangelicalism as well as his instinctive view of the
world—a 'less strait-jacketed, less censorious, more
broad-minded way of life', is the way he describes with

[19]   *Ibid.*, p. 169.
[20]   *Ibid.*, p. 149.
[21]   *Transforming of the Kirk*, p. 55.

favour the ideal of certain late Victorian Scottish Christians.[22] Quotations abound, for like his view of the Church's unity in diversity and the Christian obligation therefore to take toleration and moderation for our garment, his view of the nature of Christian faith is everywhere clear, as is evidence of his personal honesty, which, in addition to his broad understanding of the issues and careful reading of the documents, his humour and skill with the English language, give both his writing and his lectures their lasting charm, as well as their lasting importance.

[22] *Ibid.*, p. 174.

~

10
Churchman

~

Teacher and scholar though he primarily and pre-eminently was, Professor Cheyne never ceased to be a churchman. The very practical and pastoral concerns that inspired his teaching, and compelled him as a young man to prepare for the ministry, continued to occupy his thought and work to the end. He was not, that is, one of those scholar-ministers of whom Professor Shaw reminds us, who 'once they become settled in university or college … get so engrossed in the academic life that they do not have much time for exercising responsibility in the Church'.[23]

He was, for one thing, an able and active preacher. He genuinely liked to preach, in fact said that preaching was 'more rewarding in a way than teaching'. His sermons, like his lectures, were always written out (usually with a 'very rough draft' preceding), as were his prayers, 'every word of them', with the same black Parker fountain pen he used for nearly everything of importance. The problem with not having a script in preaching is that 'I feared it would go on far too long. You get side-tracked'.

---

[23] *Scottish Christianity in the Modern World*, p. 12.

But in preaching, perhaps more than in teaching, time is important: 'after twenty minutes people get restless'. In church too you have a much more diverse range of abilities than in a classroom. You have to think seriously about your audience: 'New College chapel or an evangelical congregation in the east of Scotland?' Besides, 'Wherever I've gone, whatever I've spoken on, there's always somebody who knows more than I do'. Or so he used to say, especially in his younger days. One imagines that that became less true as the years went by.

He preached often and on a wonderful variety of occasions: baptisms, weddings, funerals, dedications of churches (and at least once, of church doors), anniversaries of various sorts, as well as regular Sunday worship, frequently at the invitation of former students. And although he preached many of his sermons several times (the dates neatly recorded at the top of the first page), he never did so without rewriting them; never simply lifted them out of the file, so to speak.

The sermons are also good, very good: centred in Christ, intellectually challenging but always accessible and applicable, edifying but never sentimental, eminently suited to the occasion. It should be said that they were, as well, creative in the best sense: penetrating, and not the expected or obvious explication of the text. There is, for instance, an Advent sermon on 'The Festive Aspect of Faith'. The text is Luke 15.24 ('And they began to make merry') and the point that 'If you are inclined to opt out of all the jollifications, all the fun and games of the Christmas season, concentrating all your attention on such solemn realities as the state of your soul or the miseries of the world around us, you may be at least partially wrong. Why do I say this? Because of what we find in the Bible. Despite the dreadful evidence of human sin and folly which confronts us on every page of it, the overall picture of life which it presents is more like a wedding than a wake .... Even people's sinfulness is driven into second place by God's forgiving mercy, and the dominant message of Jesus' healing miracles could be summed up in His words to the paralytic man: "Take heart, my son; your sins are forgiven"'. Not what one learns to expect, perhaps, from an Advent sermon, but a good word for those of us inclined to take ourselves or our piety too seriously.

Or there is 'On being a Minority', a sermon first preached at Brasenose College, Oxford. Yes, Christians are a minority, Professor Cheyne acknowledged—the way, after all, is narrow—but it would be foolish to become obsessed with the fact. Moreover, there are advantages in being a minority, at least this minority: Christians are the salt of the earth, and the future, we are encouraged, is with them, 'not with the strident, triumphant majority'. It is to us that Christ gives the promise, "I will be with you always"—and 'compared with that divine companionship, who would opt for the lonely crowd?' There are warnings as well: (1) We have no right to despise the unbelieving majority (Jesus commanded His followers 'to do all they could to bring these wanderers into the fold'); and (2) 'Members of the Christian minority should never forget that the

circumstances in which they find themselves are designed
not for agonized (or gratified!) contemplation, but for
urgent action', for, 'In the end of the day, the only
worthwhile—the only worthy-reason for becoming and
continuing a Christian is that (however few or many may
agree with us) we believe the claims made for Jesus Christ
to be true, and that we commit our lives to Him'. Indeed.

In 'Strength in Weakness' we are forcefully and
eloquently reminded that we are not to be deceived by
external appearances. The Saviour of the world, after all,
'had no beauty, no majesty to catch our eyes, no grace to
attract us to him … Yet it was our afflictions he was
bearing, our pain he was bearing, our pain he endured
…'. And the Apostle Paul, as he himself tells us in 2
Corinthians, was thought by some of his converts to be a
most unimpressive character (his letters are weighty, but
he himself is a 'bit of a let-down')—to which Paul
responded: 'Yes, we are a poor lot in worldly terms; and if
it's success and splendour and a fine show of physical,
intellectual and spiritual superiority you want you'd
better look elsewhere'. For Paul was following his Master;
thus he tells the Corinthians that 'his misfortunes and
misadventures, his trials and tribulations (of which they
are so contemptuous) vindicate his apostleship rather
than disprove it. His life is a continual re-enactment of
the death that Jesus died—indeed a participation in it;
and he knows that by sharing in his Lord's death he will
share in his risen life. "When I am weak, then I am
strong."' So it must be with all who follow Christ. 'We
may not be very impressive persons. We don't think all

that much of ourselves—and nobody else thinks a great deal of us either. Perhaps we are sick, or old, or harassed or depressed; ineffective and not particularly admirable. But the light of the Cross can shine from even the most earthen vessel: Therefore, as Jesus said, "Let your light shine, that the world may see, and glorify your Father in heaven." This for those of us who may need a gentle reminder of the difference Christ makes in our mostly very ordinary lives—or by what means he makes them extraordinary.

His sermons are, as well, enviably literate, especially those given in an academic setting. In a fine homily delivered to students and faculty at the opening of session in October, 1990, entitled 'Strangers—Sojourners—Seekers—Citizens', Professor Cheyne offers needed encouragement, in particular to those far from home: 'Whatever Iliads and Odysseys, conflicts and journeyings lie ahead of you, may you be cheered and sustained (as I'm sure the folk at Ephesus were) by the realization that you are no longer passing travellers or even pilgrims, but fellow-citizens with God's people, and members of God's household'. And for this university crowd he quotes not only from 1 Chronicles, the Psalms and the Epistles to the Hebrews and Ephesians, but from the poet Edwin Muir, the historian Bernard Manning, the preacher/ theologian David Cairns, and an old student drinking song (in Latin).

I should mention one more, 'Jabez and his Sorrow', especially interesting because it deals with the same subject as does a highly-touted and widely-read devotional book which a few years ago topped the *New York Times* best seller list for weeks, *The Prayer of Jabez*. I will say only this: for its sensitivity to the nuances of the text, its understanding of the human condition from a Christian point of view, and its appreciation of the Jabez story in light of the sufferings of Christ, 'Jabez and his Sorrow' is better than *The Prayer of Jabez*.

I have spent these several pages on Professor Cheyne's preaching not only to demonstrate his commitment to the Church, but also to try to say something about *him*— for in a way, I think, his preaching may reveal more about him than even his teaching. Sermons are, after all, about the most important things, and the way a man talks about such things sheds a good deal of light on who he is—not in every case, of course, but often: the shape of his convictions, the care and passion with which he articulates them, what he emphasizes and what he does not. Preaching is not primarily an academic exercise, although the best sermons, of course, are not only articulate, but breathe deeply of concentrated study and ripened thought, not least on the text of Scripture. They are reflections of a theology lived and an acute sensitivity to men and things regarded in light of the revelation of God in Christ as given in the Old and New Testaments. They are also, of course, shaped profoundly by the preacher's own experience of God over a lifetime— theology lived, as I said. There is plenty in Professor Cheyne's sermons to reveal a preacher who not only knew and had meditated on the biblical text, but who cared deeply about what it had to say to himself and those to whom he was speaking, in their own very real and very present condition. But never, it should be added, with the slightest hint of superior knowledge or status, intellectually or spiritually, and always with an awareness that, as he put it in another of his sermons, 'our life as Christians—its comfort, its joy, its hope—depends upon, and derives from, the death (and the death-in-life of which the Cross was the culmination) of Him who alone is truly entitled to say to each of his followers, "Death was at work in me, but life in you"'.

This concern for how (and if) the Gospel was being heard in the churches is reflected similarly in remarks he made following his retirement. 'I'm becoming almost obsessed with this problem', he said about how to get people, especially younger people, to church, something he talked about frequently. There are also questions— increasingly in a society rapidly becoming secularized but wanting nonetheless the blessing of the church on their marriages or their children—about such things as baptizing the children of unchurched parents. 'A wedding is manageable, and a funeral, to my mind, is certainly manageable', he said, 'but a baptism—I don't quite know what to do about it'.

As for modern apostasy: in the late Victorian era there were many 'reverse conversions', a number well-known, often the result of intense intellectual struggle. Nowadays 'society is so secularized that people are out of [the faith] before they have a chance to reject it'. Christianity is not prominent enough that people have the opportunity to come to terms with it. 'We're moving, quite rapidly', he said, 'from indifference to hostility. It's sad that all these centuries of devotion and commitment and self-sacrifice and so on are just, it seems, forgotten'.

On the controversial topic of church music: 'I'm not on the whole thrilled with nineteenth-century hymns', he said; not much by twentieth and twenty-first century choruses either. (The tunes are 'hurdy-gurdy tunes' to a large extent.) It is the God-centred, not the individual-centred emphasis that was appealing to him. 'I find the praise very important to me', he said, mentioning Isaac Watts's 'I'll praise my Maker while I've breath', which he called 'a wonderful hymn'.

This turn in the conversation brought us back to the issue of biblical criticism, something we talked about fairly often, as it figured so largely in his own religious development as well as his academic speciality. Biblical criticism drives us to Christ, he said. Where is the centre? is the question. 'The centre for us is Christ. The person of Christ is what other religions don't have'. At the same time, it is the Church that matters. 'Christianity is not a fundamentally individual thing—certainly not'.

It is not surprising then that Professor Cheyne was involved in the administrative or organizational, as well as the devotional, life of the Church; but on his contributions there Professor Shaw's excellent summary should be the final word. 'In the courts of the Church he played a full part, whether in the Presbytery of Edinburgh, which, in recognition of his service, in 1987 elected him Moderator, or in the General Assembly .... Yet for all that, possibly his most telling contribution to the life of the Church has been the quiet and helpful guidance he has so willingly given to the many individual parish ministers (not only former students) who would come to him with their problems and never go away unattended. A convinced Presbyterian, he could nevertheless himself have made an excellent bishop! As it was, as Principal of New College, he had a special responsibility for Church of Scotland candidates for the ministry, a role to which he was admirably suited and which he fulfilled with distinction'.[24]

[24]   *Scottish Christianity in the Modern World*, p. 13.

~

11
Man of Culture

~

IN his appreciation Professor Shaw refers to his friend as, among other things, a man of culture; and it is this side of Professor Cheyne that is as interesting as any, for it is his non-professional side, what he did and was simply as himself, as it were, rather than in his role or according to his image, although of course these things are never possible to untangle.

Not unexpectedly Professor Cheyne, like his mother, was a great reader of poetry, especially the Romantics, especially Wordsworth, although Coleridge as well— 'what I know of Coleridge', he demurred, although it seemed quite a lot! His love of poetry, his serious interest in it, was reflected, for anyone who knew him, in his remarkable ability to quote it, often long passages, often in the middle of a lecture—from, yes, Wordsworth and Coleridge, of course, but Robert Burns and Milton as well, contributing to that something about his classes that made them so looked-forward-to.

A knowledge of poetry has its practical uses besides, although no one who genuinely loves poetry would list that first. It helps one write 'with grace and a sensitivity to words', as Professor Cheyne put it, a grace and sensitivity obvious in 'the elegance of his own English style', as Professor Shaw reminds us.

There were of course wider literary interests, clustered, not surprisingly (given his academic speciality), around the nineteenth century: Wordsworth and Coleridge on one end, Thomas Hardy on the other. Indeed Hardy is 'about as modern as I get', he confessed. Contemporary literature Professor Cheyne read 'hardly at all', but reread old favourites, in fact had recently reread all of both Austen and Dickens. Henry James he had read a little ('quite enjoyed'), but not Hemingway ('oh, no, I'm sorry'); Carson McCullers ('quite good') and Flannery O'Connor some ('horrible, dark stories, but a good writer'); Faulkner never ('fearsome').

It seemed obvious enough that an historian who so thoroughly enjoyed literature should be asked about his regard for historical fiction. 'It doesn't appeal to me', he admitted. There was some flirtation at Oxford with the philosophy of history, but in the end he reckoned it was a 'blind alley', at least a 'side-track'. 'You could spend your whole life agonizing about a philosophy of history and never do any history. The business of historians is to get on with history, not worry about a philosophy of history'.

What then of music, that other cultural interest nurtured in his boyhood home? Professor Shaw says of him that 'Music ... is his great love .... Gifted with an exceptional musical ear, he can identify almost anything from the classical repertoire from the first few bars—the classical repertoire, please note, for he has not many kind words for contemporary offerings'.[25] And the range, chronologically speaking: 'Again, it peters out round about the First World War. There's not much after that', he said. Favourites were Bach, Beethoven, Schubert, Dvorak, Brahms, Mozart and Haydn ('Haydn I'm very fond of'). 'Some Vaughan Williams I like, but none of this atonal stuff'. In other words, 'It pretty much stops with Stravinsky: I don't just like playing around with complexities of notes—these patterns and so on. It seems over-cerebral for me'.

As with a good deal in his life, Professor Cheyne seemed, sensibly, to be able to sort out what he liked from what he didn't like, with not a lot of bother about what perhaps he should like or what most people like. 'You've just got to recognize your sympathies and enjoy them', he said. 'I'm not ever going to really enjoy Prokofiev. I know that, so why bother?'

Jazz? 'Funnily enough, I can quite enjoy some jazz'. But not rock, 'that awful insistent thump music, which I find just odious'. Scott Joplin is 'wonderful' and his music, according to sister Mona, 'incredibly difficult', maybe because people play him too fast. 'I think [Joplin] has got a kinship with Chopin. It sounds funny, but I really do think he plumbs the depths of the piano'.

As for his own musical abilities: he made 'a joyful noise' in church but not really anywhere else. He could sight-read largely as a result of his having a wonderful music teacher in primary school who trained choirs and

---

[25]   *Scottish Christianity in the Modern World*, pp. 13–14.

had them participate in competitions, 'winning prizes at the Edinburgh Music Festival and so on'. He also played the piano, but mostly hymns, because his piano teacher, figuring he would 'never really go in for the big stuff', nonetheless 'unleashed me on the hymnody'.

In its own way, of course, Professor Cheyne's interest in literature and music, like his humour, played no small role in his teaching. It was all part of who he was, a gifted and many-sided human being as well as a superbly trained professional.

~

12

In Mufti

~

I mean here to speak very briefly about Professor Cheyne out of uniform, as it were, to say something of a more or less personal nature about him, not as professor or churchman, or writer or intellectual, or even man of culture, but simply as ordinary human being—not inappropriate, I assume, given his own eminently biographical approach to most subjects. But, as I said at the beginning, I have no interest in anything 'intimate' or (for goodness sake!) 'psychological'. Nonetheless there are aspects of Professor Cheyne's life that are, well, simply interesting, apart from anything else, and may contribute in any case to a more well-rounded portrait—as would be true of any of us.

I might begin by saying that in fact I do not think I have ever seen Professor Cheyne, in the literal sense, out of uniform. I have never, not even in a photograph, seen him in anything but a suit, at least a sports jacket and dress trousers, and never without a tie. Once I asked if he always wore a jacket and tie. Without hesitation he answered simply, 'Yes'. But then it would be hard to imagine him in anything else; and, according to friends and family, he had rather a penchant for nice ties and good clothes generally.

Nor, perhaps, did he require very much of anything else. He did not go in for 'exercise' of the contemporary sort; at least there were no athletic interests—'absolutely not'. He had apparently done some cross-country running in high school, and some climbing and 'lots of hill walking', especially on holiday, throughout most of his life, but as for sports like squash or golf: 'couldn't be bothered'. The only exercise he had when he was teaching in Edinburgh, he said, was walking to college, but then that was probably a good deal more than most people, driving cars, had. He enjoyed 'pretty fine' health most of his life, except about the time of Mona's final illness. Two heart attacks in 1999 were probably the result of worrying about her condition.

In his youth the bulk of his holidays were taken in the Highlands, near Inverness, the Black Isle, Munlochy. In those days family holidays were generally taken, as was the custom, in manses, father preaching, mother cooking. As a young lecturer Alec holidayed on the continent, in Germany and Switzerland, motoring down to the south of England with a friend, putting the car on the plane and flying to Zurich, from where they drove to Basel and other destinations, Italy being a favourite. For ten years at least he and Mona stayed for a week in self-catering cottages in the Lake District.

He travelled to the United States a number of times, and to a wide variety of places there, from as far north and west as Alaska to as far south and west as Tucson; but also the mid-west, the east and north-east. In fact it was in Anchorage in 1976 where he learned that his father was mortally ill. He had gone to Alaska to speak to young ministers who had been brought in from remote places to hear him, but because of his father's condition had to pack the lectures into a short period and fly home. The autumn semester of 1972 he spent at Wooster College in Ohio on an exchange teaching arrangement. (I remember vividly his first day in class after his return to New College when he wondered out loud how much of his Scottish accent he had lost in America. To reassure himself he paused and uttered 'Auchtermuchty'—'just wanted to see if I could still pronounce that', he said, to the delight of his students, especially the Americans.) His longest trip to the U.S. was in 1986 following his retirement: Buffalo (New York), Richmond (Virginia), Swarthmore (Pennsylvania), Fargo (North Dakota) and Seattle (Washington). He found the people of America 'just incredibly welcoming and hospitable'. He never lectured on the continent, but, in addition to the United States, in New Zealand—and wherever he went the subject was almost always Scottish Church history.

Professor Cheyne never learned to drive a car, and, I suppose, never really needed to. When Mona was alive *she* drove—the little VW in which she transported her harpsichord to and from performances. In fact that is how she chose her cars, he said: she measured to see if they would take a harpsichord!

He did learn something of the computer, however, enough certainly to use it for word-processing, 'like a typewriter', although he was never absolutely convinced it was all it was made out to be. 'People say to me, "Isn't the computer marvellous; you can move paragraphs around, and so on". I've never wanted to move a paragraph in my life', he said. Nor did he compose on the computer. The first draft was always pen on paper; the ideas, he once told me, 'just come out of the end of the pen'.

Professor Cheyne's was, it seems, a wonderfully ordered life, focused, not attempting to do everything, and therefore productive. There were the occasional diversions, though. He admitted to having a sweet tooth—biscuits and pastries of all sorts at the very regular tea breaks (coffee only in the morning)—but his 'staple diet' was chocolate and his favourite Cadbury's Dairy Milk.

~

13

Liberal Historiography

~

BEHIND and beneath everything else, however, are what for me the equally interesting parts of any man's life, namely, the intellectual and religious antecedents, or more specifically, what I called earlier Professor Cheyne's rootedness in 'the tradition of liberal historiography' referred to by Brown and Newlands, and the liberal Evangelicalism mentioned by Professor Shaw.

For an understanding of Professor Cheyne's indebtedness to the tradition of liberal historiography I am myself indebted to Stewart J. Brown, successor to Professor Cheyne in the Chair and currently Professor of Ecclesiastical History in Edinburgh. Professor Brown was most generous with his expertise, and it is a pleasure to acknowledge that much of what I say in this section I learned from him.

The phrase 'liberal historiography' refers in part to the tradition of historical writing that flourished in Britain in the nineteenth-century and included such historians as T. B. Macaulay, A. E. Freeman, Charles Kingsley, J. A. Froude and Lord Acton, as well as such twentieth-century writers as Richard Pares and George Kitson Clark. 'If asked to elaborate further', Professor Brown said, 'I would add that the tradition had its roots in the Enlightenment historians, and especially the great Scottish historian, William Robertson'. Professor Cheyne himself often mentioned the influence of Bernard Manning as well.

To be specific, the tradition of liberal historiography would mean at least the following:

First, an emphasis on human freedom, as opposed to deterministic historiographical traditions, such as Marx's historical dialectic or Karl Pearson's Social Darwinism. In other words, for historians in the liberal tradition, individual human beings, as free agents, shape their own history. We are influenced by our environment and physical limitations, of course, but our history is not ultimately determined by environment or class conflict or race. Our ideas and efforts matter.

That is not to say that the liberal historian necessarily discounts the role of providence in history. It is simply that in modesty he does not presume to *know* the actions of providence in history. Professor Cheyne, for instance, very consciously made sure that providence was not seen as a factor in his Church history courses. Or rather, perhaps, that the role of providence was a question to wrestle with like any other question, and thus was Church history to be studied in the same way as any other kind of history. In other words, just because it was Church history did not mean that it required (though it might tempt or invite) 'providential explanations' in its analysis.

Former Free Church Manse at Keig
where William Robertson Smith was raised
April 1994

Mona's 70th birthday

The study at Oaklea, Peebles, 1996

The Summer Institute, St Andrews
June 1997

Stobo Kirk

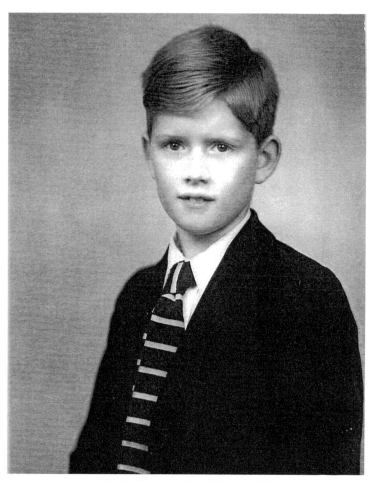

A. C. Cheyne, about 11 years old
Probably Kirkcaldy, c.1935

Cheyne family

A. C. Cheyne's mother and sister Mona

Rev. Alexander Cheyne, 1920s

Rev. Alexander Cheyne C. 1940

A. C. Cheyne 1956

In the Army "with my platoon"
A. C. Cheyne is the tall one, front row centre

The Rainy Hall, New College, 1975–1980

New College classroom 1970s

Oaklee, Peebles 1985

Liberal historiography would, then, secondly, emphasize the importance of individual actors in history. History is not to be regarded as solely about 'large human collections' (as Professor Brown calls them)—social classes or races or nations—but recognizes that history is a human story, often a story about individual men or women. Thus a great deal of Professor Cheyne's historical writing was biographical, as we have seen. Appropriately, then, much of Professor Cheyne's prose style was narrative. Indeed he was 'a master of narration (very much in the tradition of the great William Robertson), ,says Professor Brown.

The liberal historian believes, thirdly, in the development of institutions combining liberty under law; moreover, that individual human nature can be elevated when men and women participate in institutions such as parliament, voluntary societies, universities, local governments and churches. For his part, Professor Cheyne, interestingly, also believed firmly that churches must have spiritual independence from the state, and his inclination was towards voluntary churches, despite being a leading member of the Church of Scotland—all of this best documented, perhaps, says Professor Brown, in his writings on the Disruption.

Or so, at least, it seems, although on this subject Professor Cheyne was certainly not dogmatic. The parties in the Ten Years' Conflict he describes as, on the one hand, 'the Moderates—reasonable men, accommodating and down-to-earth, the lesser descendants of those eighteenth-century giants, William Robertson and his

friends, who had made Edinburgh one of the centres of
the enlightened world ...' and 'the reinvigorated Popular
party, on the other hand, strong in the enthusiasm,
demonstrative piety and crusading spirit of the religious
revival associated with the names of Wesley, Whitefield
and Wilberforce ...'. The latter party, he says, 'had
already annexed the challenging title of "Evangelical" and
was now poised to take over the direction of religious
affairs from its allegedly effete, reactionary and worldly-
minded adversaries'.[26]

As for temper, disposition, spirit: his sympathies seem
clearly to lie with the 'reasonable men', the
'accommodating and down-to-earth' Moderates, not with
the annexing and assertive Evangelicals. As for the
consequence, however: he seems to agree that no matter
how over-enthusiastic and impatient the Popular party,
their cause was the right one, and disestablishment the
proper result. He seems to agree, that is, with Owen
Chadwick: 'quietness and patience and persuasion are no
less Christian virtues than is heroic sacrifice of stipends
on high principle'. 'Nevertheless the headship of Christ is
that without which churches may as well be swept aside
into heaps of rubble or converted into gymnasia'.[27] Here
Professor Cheyne's own moderation allows him to view
means and ends with remarkable balance, not to say a
hint of tentativeness; preferring the Moderate means he
nonetheless approves the Evangelical end.

[26]   *Studies in Scottish Church History*, p. 107.
[27]   *Ibid.*, p. 119.

Fourthly, liberal historians believe in human progress, that the movement of society is towards greater liberty, social justice and equality; that despite wars, famines, and a multitude of other man-made tragedies, humanity is moving forward. I suppose it would be difficult to document this in Professor Cheyne's writing, but it seems to me to be the natural complement of the other elements of the liberal historiography suggested above. It was certainly consistent with his general outlook, in any case: his personal liberality, for instance, his general optimism, his willingness to believe the best of people. Of course, as with most of us, this may well have been in him the confluence of a considered point of view and his temperament, what he believed and what he simply was. And like most of us, even his optimism occasionally gave way to 'a certain despondence about humanity's prospects', as Professor Brown puts it.

What is not difficult to document, however, is his firm conviction that, along with its other, perhaps more spiritual, ministries, the Church must be committed to the cause of economic and social justice. His criticisms of Thomas Chalmers's programmes for the amelioration of the poor in his essay on Chalmers in *Studies in Scottish Church History*[28] and his chapter on 'The Social Revolution' in *The Transforming of the Kirk*,[29] spell that out in no uncertain terms.

Finally, a liberal historiography believes that ideas matter. It takes intellectual history seriously; it believes in

[28] *Studies in Scottish Church History*, p. 79ff.
[29] *Transforming of the Kirk*, pp. 110ff.

the progress of human thought. That is, it does not see humanity as simply the pawn of economic or social forces or think that ideas are nothing more than the 'superstructure' by means of which the dominant social classes exercise power, as certain Marxist historians might have it. Professor Cheyne would never accept, for instance, that churches are simply the means by which feudal landowners or the industrial bourgeoisie exercised control over the lower social orders. No, ideas have the power to be independent of, indeed to alter, the course of economic or social history.

These, briefly, are the influences of 'the tradition of liberal historiography' in Professor Cheyne's writing. As intimated above, the tradition suited him. One can hardly imagine his approach to history, like his temperament, as anything other than liberal in the best sense.

~

14

Liberal Evangelicalism

~

PROFESSOR Cheyne's Liberal Evangelicalism may be more difficult to get hold of. In fact, at one point in a conversation about this he said, 'I wouldn't make too much of it, because once you start on it, it's going to be very difficult to extricate yourself and define exactly what you're after'. The problem for me was that I was thinking in American categories, and 'Liberal Evangelicalism' seemed an oxymoron, which, in the Scottish context, it was not. 'Evangelical' in Scotland in Professor Cheyne's formative years meant warmly evangelistic, concerned with 'presenting people with Jesus', 'making the Bible come alive, and so on'. 'Liberal', on the other hand, meant simply not fundamentalist, and that meant, primarily, not taking all of the Bible literally. 'It meant that you did not believe every word of Scripture as being historically correct'. So, whatever one might think about the first couple of chapters of Genesis, say, there were still rallies and altar calls, missionary enthusiasm, and the frequent assertion that, 'What we need is revival'. Of his father, for instance, Professor Cheyne said: 'he looked upon himself as an Evangelical, without any doubt', but he 'never was a fundamentalist'. Even though he could quote the entire Shorter Catechism from memory, 'Doctrinal statements and confessional utterances didn't seem to figure very largely in [his] approach to things. He was saturated in the text of the Bible, but I don't remember his using the phrase "substitutionary atonement", for example—never ever. He was quite convinced about original sin, but, again, he didn't preach it'.

Similarly with matters of science: 'My father was not always fulminating against either those who supported Darwinism or those who opposed it', Professor Cheyne recalled. In general, the liberal-conservative war was 'never the issue in Scotland that it was in the U.S., never the extremes on either side'. This may go some way to explaining the enthusiasm of men like Henry Drummond, popularizer of evolutionary theory, and George Adam Smith, Old Testament critic, for the evangelistic fervour of Moody and Sankey: there was apparently no contradiction for them in holding to either historical-critical views of the Bible or Darwinian views of origins and a warmly evangelical faith.

So 'Liberal Evangelicalism' had to do with a very definite commitment to the Evangel, even to evangelism and a personal relationship to Christ, but had a looser grip on issues of historical or scientific import, at least devotionally speaking. Such an ordering of priorities had the effect of relegating questions of biblical inerrancy or the authorship of the Pentateuch, for instance, to a place of secondary importance; or as John Tulloch reminded his hearers at Crathie in his sermon on 'Religion and

Theology', 'the welfare of the soul is not determined by theology and its answer to such problems as "the antiquity of man, the age of Genesis or the earth, the origin and the authority of the several books of Scripture"'. Of these things, he said, he could not be sure. What he could know, however, was that 'I am a spiritual being, and have spiritual needs craving to be satisfied, and that God is a spiritual power above me, of whom Christ is the revelation .... These things', he said, 'are facts which I may know or not know, irrespective of such matters'. Tulloch's last word, on the issue, as Professor Cheyne called it, is 'a summons to rigorous inquiry on the theological level, together with quiet receptivity on the religious level'.[30]

On its more strictly intellectual or academic side, Liberal Evangelicalism could be summed up, as Professor Cheyne sums it up in reference to John Baillie, under three heads: 'deference to the methods and findings of natural science, wariness of all creedal and confessional statements, and devotion to the use of literary and historical criticism of the Bible'.[31] Liberal Evangelicalism, then, was characterized by attitudes regarding both devotion and scholarship, and perhaps most importantly, the relationship between the two.

[30] *Studies in Scottish Church History*, p. 148.
[31] *Transforming of the Kirk*, p. 200; also *Studies in Scottish Church History*, p. 210.

~

15
Influences

~

W HO then were the influences in Professor Cheyne's
life, intellectually and religiously? He mentioned
first his Christian home, especially as a teenager,
particularly when he began to realize how many people
were not Christians, and how many of them were
exceedingly able and impressive thinkers. Such were
Thomas Hardy and Bertrand Russell, whom he read in
the Kirkcaldy library ('where I came up against the
modern view of the world'), admired not for their
agnosticism, of course, but for their writing and
penetrating intellects. 'These were sort of contrary
influences', he said. On the positive side and even more
influential were the Baillie brothers, John and Donald.
Donald Baillie's best friend was J. Y. (Jack) Campbell,
Professor Cheyne's mother's brother; this was the family
connection mentioned earlier, and no doubt a large part
of the reason for the Baillies' considerable importance,
which we have seen throughout.

There was also D. S. Cairns. 'People like Cairns were
able to describe the Christian faith in a most attractive
way', Professor Cheyne recalled. This was especially true

of books like Cairns' *The Faith that Rebels*, an attempt to get a solution to the problem of the miracles of Jesus that was neither Traditionalist nor Modernist; also an attempt to put together science and religion—which at the time must have had enormous appeal for a young Christian of intellectual bent. 'When I was getting interested in theology, several liberal Anglicans also had quite an effect on me', he said. Canon Streeter, for example, was 'a wonderful apologist for the faith'. Also William Temple, who, along with Canon Streeter was 'flourishing in my youth'. Thus were Streeter and Temple and Baillie 'three strong influences'.

He also mentioned Professor A. E. Taylor, his teacher of moral philosophy at Edinburgh, 'a most distinguished Christian thinker', and Professor Vivian Hunter Galbraith, one of his 'real influences', who made history 'intoxicatingly interesting'. A 'very distinguished medievalist', Galbraith 'taught me not only history but the art of communication'. Sadly, Galbraith left Edinburgh in Alec's second year there to become Director of the Historical Institute in London. Later he was Regius Professor of History in Oxford. Based in Oriel College, he was 'probably responsible for my admission there'.

~

16
Coleridge and Burns

~

THE most profound insights into Professor Cheyne's view of the world ('my *Weltanshaung*, to use a word beloved of John Baillie') may come, however, in a couple of lectures he gave on his favourite poets, Samuel Taylor Coleridge and Robert Burns. Nor is this entirely surprising, given his love of literature and his appreciation of the power of literature to plumb the depths of human experience. These lectures, 'the best things I have produced', he said, 'may give you some insight into *me* if not into the people I admire (for very different reasons)'—and it is, of course, the reasons for his admiration that tell us something about the man.

In Coleridge we have the remarkable combination of a sublime poet, a seminal mind (as John Stewart Mill described him), and what Professor Cheyne calls 'a peculiarly engaging person', according to Coleridge's friend William Wordsworth, 'the most wonderful man I have ever known'. His imaginative genius is evidenced by his 'ever-memorable poems, chief among them that magical trio, "The Rime of the Ancient Mariner", "Christabel" and "Kubla Khan"'; but there is as well, in tribute to the originality of his intellect, 'a veritable library of political, philosophical and theological writings— disorganized, obscure, incomplete and flawed in many respects, yet at the same time extraordinarily stimulating and profound'. Add in his peculiarly engaging personality and his spiritual longing and we may begin to appreciate how Thomas Carlyle, 'whose over-all attitude to him was far from friendly', says Professor Cheyne, could write that Coleridge 'had, especially among young, inquiring men, a higher than literary, a kind of prophetic or magician character. He was thought to hold, he alone in England, the key of German and other Transcendentalisms; he knew the sublime secret of believing by "the reason" what "the understanding" had been obliged to fling out as incredible; and could still, after Hume and Voltaire had done their best and worst with him, profess himself an orthodox Christian .... A sublime man; who alone, in those dark days, had saved his crown of spiritual manhood; escaping from the black materialisms, and deluges, with "God, Freedom, Immortality" still his: a king of men'.

There is plenty in Coleridge to admire all right: perspicacity, perseverance, courage, largeness of soul. But the question Professor Cheyne wants primarily to attempt to answer in this lecture is, 'What may a resolute seeker after God learn from one whose whole life—to quote Charles Lamb again—was driven by "a hunger for eternity"?' That this was the important question is itself pertinent. So are Professor Cheyne's answers, what he considers 'among Coleridge's most valuable contributions to the quest for religious truth and spiritual fulfilment'.

He lists first Coleridge's distinction between 'Reason' and 'Understanding', Reason being (quoting one commentator on Coleridge) 'the eye of the spirit, the faculty whereby the spiritual reality is spiritually discerned', and Understanding, 'the science of a phenomenon'. While Understanding has 'a wide and legitimate field of activity'—measurement, analysis, classification 'and all other processes of natural science'— and while it 'controls our lives on the practical, routine level', it 'begins to err when it encroaches on the spheres where reason alone is valid, when it pretends to erect its limited theories into absolute laws, mistaking a technique of experiment or a method of classification for an exhaustive account of reality'. And this, for Coleridge, the same commentator tells us, 'was precisely what had happened in the eighteenth century'. The result, says Professor Cheyne, was 'materialism, determinism, atheism and a host of other evils with which we are only too familiar still'. He concludes: 'It is not hard to see how the Coleridgeian distinction between Reason and Understanding ... helped to free many of his followers in early-Victorian Britain from the tyranny of "science, falsely so called"'. Finally, he asks, 'have we something to learn from it even now?'

The second of Coleridge's contributions to the quest for religious truth and spiritual fulfilment, argues Professor Cheyne, is what he calls Coleridge's 're-interpretation of Biblical authority', by which is meant his rejection of the doctrine that the Bible is an 'inspired and *inerrant* compendium of divine truths, equally authoritative in all its parts'. Coleridge rejected this view, says Professor Cheyne, for two reasons primarily. First, because in his judgment 'it failed to reckon with the facts as they were being uncovered by literary and historical scholarship' and, second, because 'its effect was to obscure the real power of the Bible to touch the heart and speak to the human condition at its deepest level'. He then quotes the famous passage from *Confessions of an Inquiring Spirit*: 'Why should I not believe the Scriptures [to be] throughout dictated, in word and thought, by an infallible Intelligence? ... eagerly and earnestly do I answer: For every reason that makes me prize and revere these Scriptures; prize them, love them, revere them, beyond all other books! ... Because the doctrine in question petrifies at once the whole body of Holy Writ with all its harmonies .... This breathing organism ... turns at once into ... a hollow passage for a voice, a voice that mocks the voices of many men, and speaks in their names, and yet is but one voice and the same', concluding: 'in the Bible there is more that finds me than I have experienced in all other books put together; that the words of the Bible find me at greater depths of my being; and that whatever finds me brings with it an irresistible evidence of its having proceeded from the Holy Spirit'. Professor Cheyne's comment: 'There are many who would contend that his arguments did much to strengthen thinking Christians against the shock which critical methods of study were about to inflict on all the

Churches'. And again: 'Have we still something to learn from him?'

The third of Coleridge's contributions Professor Cheyne calls 'his enriching vision of the world—its splendour, its misery, its supernatural dimensions', and here, 'inevitably', he says, 'we turn to his greatest work, "The Rime of the Ancient Mariner"'. Quoting extensively, Professor Cheyne attempts to show why 'there cannot be many places in literature where the mystery, the terror, the beauty and wonder of the world have been more memorably expressed than in this poem'. He refers, as well, to Coleridge's emphasis, 'so congenial to the men and women of today', on 'the vital bond between human beings and the animal creation'. But it is what the poem has to say about sin and redemption 'which must above all concern us here'; and what the poem has to say Professor Cheyne discusses in terms of five categories, all of course supported by full references to the text: the fact of sin, the infection of sin, the fearful consequences of sin, the need to expiate sin, and the presence of grace and the possibility of Redemption. He concludes by quoting Basil Willey's comment that 'if we live with [Coleridge] long enough, share his valiant struggles for Faith against heavy odds, and watch his final attainment of it, we shall be inclined to see him ... as the prototype of those ... who have sought to renovate the Faith, not by re-stating it intellectually, but by living it out into reality themselves'. Coleridge, says Professor Cheyne, was 'the seeker—and finder—of faith'; not perfect by any means, indeed 'a flawed and tragic' genius, plagued by drug addiction, disappointment in marriage and fatherhood, as well as physical ailment and financial woe. 'Yet', quoting Walter Jackson Bate of Harvard, 'the inner record of his soul is one of ever-increasing faith, acceptance, and spiritual joy. ... [He was] a man hampered, in the physical world, by every ill, but spiritually a giant, and an adventurer in all the countries of the imagination'.

If all of this tells us something about Professor Cheyne, as well as about Coleridge, as he said it does, what is it? I said in the introduction that this was no 'intimate portrait', certainly nothing like a 'study' or an 'analysis'. All such is entirely out of place here. But since we have his invitation, we are allowed perhaps to proceed, albeit 'very diffidently' (as he characterized the way he approached Coleridge's contributions to the quest for religious truth and spiritual fulfilment) towards a couple of tentative conclusions.

There is first Professor Cheyne's deep sympathy for Coleridge's view of Scripture, a sympathy reinforced any number of times over the years in comments formal and informal. The doctrine of biblical inerrancy obviously satisfied neither his mind nor his spirit; and it was no doubt this personal coming to terms with the issue that informed his handling of it in his work on the Scottish Church in the nineteenth century, where it played such a pivotal role.

The same might be said of his appreciation for Coleridge's distinction between Understanding and Reason, especially with regard to 'the tyranny of "science, falsely so called"', as he puts it. For along with 'the shock which critical methods of study [of the Bible] were about to inflict on all the churches', there was also the shock of an exclusively scientific view of the world, 'resulting in materialism, determinism, atheism and a host of other evils with which we are only too familiar still'. These things too he had had to grapple with, intellectually and spiritually, and Coleridge had come to his aid.

As significant as these issues are in the religious journey of any thinking twentieth-century Christian, not to mention their special relevance to one whose academic interests had come to rest in the Church in the nineteenth century, I wonder if Coleridge's attraction for Professor Cheyne might not also have to do with aspects of Coleridge's life and thought that are more subtle or spiritual, but no less real. I mean, for instance, Coleridge's understanding that the world is a dangerous place and that faith is fragile; that sin is real, around us and in us, and that while most of us enjoy an abundance of gladness and goodness, we have our share of disappointment, failure and grief, often enough as the result of our own doing. I mean, in other words, a sense that faith, too, is sometimes precarious as well as enduring.

At this point, it seems to me—and here I go very diffidently indeed—we may get close to something in Professor Cheyne that may be difficult to see, just as difficult to describe, but perhaps central to who he was. In the introductory paragraph to his lecture on Coleridge he remarked that 'There is a tendency these days to assume that Christian faith and mediocrity—safe but boring, worthy but unadventurous—go together'. He went on to say that no one had called such an assumption into question more than Coleridge. Was there in Professor Cheyne a similar adventurousness of mind and spirit, an adventurousness that understood that genuine faith is neither safe nor boring, that like Abraham it risks going out, not knowing where it is to go; and although it is a faith that on its intellectual or academic side both stimulates and requires theological formulation—thank God for the rich theological heritage of the Christian Church which he knew so well—it is not a faith that in its working out is *essentially* theological? Or as Basil Willey said of Coleridge, he was one of those who 'sought to renovate the Faith, not by re-stating it but by living it out into reality themselves'—and that means, not least, adventuresomeness, risk, perhaps terror, certainly the possibility of depths as well as heights. These are precious matters, I know; nor do I mean to give the impression that I understand them very well myself, only that I imagine that Professor Cheyne might have.

It was also said of Coleridge that was 'an adventurer in all the countries of the imagination'. Have we here, too, a comment on Professor Cheyne? As I read his explication of 'The Rime of the Ancient Mariner'—the apparent ease with which he interpreted the text, and the enjoyment he seemed to get from doing it—I began to appreciate a little, I think, of how perfectly natural it was that his first academic interest should have been English and his life-long love literature. I do not know, of course, but could it be that the relative scarcity of scholarly publications from his pen which Professor Shaw mentions—this scarcity is due not only to his perfectionism (as Professor Shaw calls it), but as well to a kind of creativity that belongs more to the writer than the academic historian? Again, it is only a surmise, but maybe one of the reasons he did not publish more, yet his lectures and sermons are so many and so good, was that teaching and preaching allowed him a certain imaginative freedom that more strictly technical academic writing did not. Maybe that is why research did not come more easily for him: it was not creative enough. These, as I said, are delicate and precious matters. I do not want to presume too much or push too hard. They are things only hinted at, but hinted at nonetheless.

To the extent that things are hinted at in Professor Cheyne's lecture on Coleridge they are limned in the boldest strokes in his lecture on Burns. An admirer but by no means a worshipper of Burns, he could abide (or maybe here I should say thole!) neither the attacks on Burns (and the Scots) by the supercilious Matthew Arnold ('that snob of snobs') nor 'that mindless show-biz, Moira Anderson and Kenneth MacKellar cult of "Rabbie Burns", the haggis and the thistle which amuse and disgust the onlooker and would have astonished Burns himself'.

At the same time he readily acknowledges that there is plenty in Burns *not* to admire: 'Those of us who are proud of him are not proud of *all* of him'; 'We must admit that, great poet as he was, there are whole areas of experience which he did not touch, and for which we must turn elsewhere'; ' His non-Christian Deism, to most of us here, seems shallow and lacking in the one thing needful'; 'He contributed not a little to the crazy adulation of drink and drunkenness which has made Scottish conviviality a byword among the nations'.

What he did admire, however, he declares in language almost as uncompromising as that which he quotes from the poet himself. Burns was, first of all, 'a phrasemaker par excellence (notably for matching words and music in a way equalled only by Schubert)'. He was also a patriot, 'a lover of his country, its places and its people, and a robust hater of its enemies', who 'deplored the self-seeking venality of Scottish politicians, at the time of the Union, in words which some would use about George Younger or George Cunningham or Sir Alec Douglas-Home today'.

But Burns is 'more than a patriot: he is a democrat'—and here we get very near, I think, to Professor Cheyne's deeper, and Christian, sensibilities. In the concluding verse of 'Does Haughty Gaul Invasion Threat?' Burns, he says, 'cocked a snook at all the Fascists of his day with these magnificently balanced sentiments':

> Who will not sing *God save the King*
> Shall hang as high's the steeple;
> But while we sing *God save the King*
> We'll ne'er forget the people!

'In the end of the day, it was to the underprivileged that [Burns's] heart went out,' Professor Cheyne reminds us, 'and he shared their hyper-sensitive pride'. Character, not wealth or status, was for Burns the best criterion by which to judge a man, for 'even so far as happiness goes, between rich and poor', he says, 'there isn't much to

choose'. For as Burns puts it in 'Epistle to Davie, a
Brother Poet':

> The honest heart that's free frae a'
>   Intended fraud or guile,
> However Fortune kicks the ba',
>   Has ay some cause to smile;
> ... ...
> If happiness hae not her seat
>   An' centre in the breast,
> We may be wise, or rich, or great,
>   But never can be blest!
>   Nae treasures nor pleasures
>   Could make us happy lang;
>   The heart ay's the part ay
>   That makes us right or wrang.

This concern for the underprivileged that Professor
Cheyne so admired in Burns is not unrelated to Burns's
genius as a humorist and a satirist, in no small part, of
course, because the humour often enough comes in his
portrayal, and his defence, of the down and out, and his
satire at the expense of the self-righteous. 'I have often
courted the acquaintance of that part of mankind
commonly known by the ordinary phrase of
"blackguards", further than was consistent with the safety
of my character', Burns wrote; but also, 'I have often
observed in the course of my experience of human life
that every man, even the worst, has something good
about him'. And it is an over-concern for precisely the
safety of one's character that was frequently the subject of
Burns's humour, and his satire. 'The Jolly Beggars', for
instance, the result of 'a foray into the haunts of
Ayrshire's submerged tenth: a visit to Poosie Nansie's

establishment in down-town Mauchline—a doss-house, drinking-den, near-brothel', consists of 'the disreputable drinking songs sung by Poosie Nansie's clients, the dregs of society'. 'The miracle is', says Professor Cheyne, 'that by the end of it we find ourselves sorely tempted to join in choruses which would do credit to the terracing at Ibrox or the post-rugby changing room'. Then, quoting the chorus of 'The Drinking Song' from 'The Jolly Beggars', in which (according to anthologist Louis Untermeyer) Burns 'treats the whole world of morality as though its existence were mythical':

> A fig for those by law protected!
>   Liberty's a glorious feast,
> Courts for cowards were erected,
>   Churches built to please the priest!

Professor Cheyne, perhaps in partial (but only partial!) acknowledgement of Burns's intemperate language, comments: 'Shocking yes—but perhaps a salutary shock to those among us who are over-much in thrall to our Super-Egos, too tightly buttoned up to escape Pharisaism!'

It is sanctimony, pose, cant that takes a thrashing here, and along with it, inauthenticity, dullness, and stagnation:[32]

> O ye douce folk that live by rule,
> Grave, tideless-blooded, calm an' cool,
> Compar'd wi you—O fool! fool! fool!
>   How much unlike!
> Your hearts are just a standing pool,
>   Your lives a dyke!

[32] From 'Epistle to James Smith'.

'A satirist of genius', Burns' 'attacks on conventional righteousness and the extravagances of old fashioned Calvinism probably helped to turn the theological tide in eighteenth-century Scotland and still have a cutting edge today', Professor Cheyne argues. 'Read, for instance, "To a Louse", and Easter bonnets at St Giles or St John's, Crammond or Colinton, will never be quite the same for you again! Or "Holy Willie's Prayer", that lethal onslaught on self-righteousness, hypocrisy and the Westminster doctrine of predestination. But, above all', Professor Cheyne advises, 'read the "Addresses to the Unco' Guid, or the Rigidly Righteous", in which satire eventually rises above itself and is sublimated into a moving summons to self-criticism and compassion ...'. Then, after quoting those contemptuous lines addressed to 'Ye high, exalted, virtuous dames, / Tied up in godly laces', which end with the admonition,

> Who made the heart, 'tis He alone
> Decidedly can try us:
> He knows each chord, its various tone,
> Each spring, its various bias:
> Then at the balance let's be mute,
> We never can adjust it;
> What's done we partly may compute,
> But know not what's resisted.

he concludes: 'Burns never, I suggest, got nearer than in those lines to one of the central emphases of Christian piety'.

Finally, Burns was, Professor Cheyne tells us, a lover; 'and when all's said and done, it is his poems of love and friendship that we value the most'. But love *and* friendship, for although (in a concession to Matthew Arnold who claimed that 'Burns is a beast'), he acknowledges that Burns '*could* be a beast where women were concerned', he reminds us that 'his genius for friendship is sometimes forgotten'. Still, he says, 'it is the story of his relations with women ... that rivets our attention and gave us some of the most exquisite love songs in the language': the 'songs of rapture and passion', the 'songs of gentle protective love', of parting love and love in old age. He closes his meditation on Burns by quoting the reflections of David Daiches on 'what is perhaps the best-known of all Burns's songs—a song not of sexual love but of friendship, "Auld Lang Syne"'.

It is perhaps no great revelation to learn that we discover something about a man from his sermons. It may be somewhat more surprising to learn as much about him as we do from his exegesis of his favourite poets. When we discover who those poets are in Professor Cheyne's case, and what he says about them, however, we may begin to see why he said that his lectures on them 'may give you some insight into *me* if not the people I admire'. There is Coleridge's imagination and intellectual acuity combined with his magnanimous soul; his apprehension of Christian faith not primarily as doctrinal but experimental; the genius by which, against what he believed lifeless religious dogmatism on the one hand and soulless scientific materialism on the other, he 'saved his crown of spiritual manhood'; the invigorating adventurousness of his Christian faith—these things Professor Cheyne admired.

There is also Burns's gift for matching words and music; but more his love of his country, even more its people, especially the poor and voiceless whose goodness and character he sang; his exuberant humour and cutting satire, most telling when unleashed against numbing conventionality and sham religion; his genius for friendship and rendering immortal the rapture and ache of love—these too Professor Cheyne admired and spoke of with enthusiasm, allowing us to see mirrored in Burns, perhaps, as well as in Coleridge, something of his own soul.

Interesting too is that both Coleridge's and Burns's personal lives were on the whole tragic. But of course it is not Coleridge's drug addiction or Burns's drunkenness and infidelity that is admirable. What may be admirable, however, is that out of such tragedy, doubtless because of it, there came not only blessing for the rest of us but (in Coleridge's case at least) redemption and faith and even joy—and that of course is an eminently Christian understanding of things, as Professor Cheyne's sermons also make clear.

In Professor Cheyne we have a son of the manse, a notable teacher and scholar, a distinguished preacher and Moderator of Edinburgh Presbytery, lifelong a man of culture whose career was shaped by education at the finest universities and, thereafter, as University Professor of Ecclesiastical History and Principal of New College, an almost continual immersion in intellectual and academic concerns—that is, someone whose life was not precisely ordinary, but who was nonetheless tuned to the affairs of ordinary life and had thought caringly about the men and women whose lives were very ordinary indeed. He was, in other words, both a Christian scholar and a Christian man. One can understand then his sympathy for both the Coleridge of 'The Rime of the Ancient Mariner' and the Coleridge of *Confessions of an Inquiring Spirit* as well as the Coleridge of 'flawed and tragic genius'; his sympathy too for the lyrical ploughman of Ayrshire.

Finally, it is not without significance, in my view, that he referred, on more than one occasion, to these lectures (and not his better-known historical writing) as 'the best things I have produced'. He did not give reasons for his judgment; but I wonder if it may have had something to do not only with his deep personal affinity for the themes the literature dealt with, but no less the imaginative and spiritual insights it required of him for its explication. That is to say that in these lectures he may have experienced something of the creative fulfilment of the poet himself.

~

17

Conclusion: Piety and Learning

~

T HE most fitting way to conclude these remarks on the life and work of Professor Cheyne may be to reflect for a moment on the motif that is implicit in almost everything that has been said so far, namely, the relationship between the religious and the academic life, or as he put it himself, 'the essential unity of piety and learning'.[33]

While he never addressed the issue on its formal or philosophical side—never took up, for instance, the question of how believing might be related to knowing—he nonetheless wrote a good deal about similar and complementary issues in his characteristically biographical way; that is, by means of commentary on the lives of Christian scholars he admired.

Two essays stand out in this regard: 'Piety and Learning: Three Edinburgh Exemplars'[34] and the first of two pieces on the Baillie brothers, 'John and Donald Baillie: A Biographical Introduction'.[35] In 'Piety and

---

[33] *Studies in Scottish Church History*, p. 202.
[34] *Ibid.*, pp. 33ff.
[35] *Ibid.*, pp. 237ff.

Learning' he begins by acknowledging that 'We are accustomed these days to think and talk of our universities as secular institutions in a pluralist society. So no doubt they are; yet surely it is important to recall how much the Christian religion has had to do with their origins and subsequent history'.[36]

This is certainly true of the Scottish Universities, Edinburgh in particular. The evidence is the lives of its worthies. Its first teacher and principal was Robert Rollock (c. 1555–99), a 'round-headed, reddish-haired youngster, still in his twenties but with a reputation for godliness and good learning'[37] who 'seems, by all accounts, to have been an especially effective *teacher*, genuinely interested in his students and ever desirous of finding the best way to communicate with them'.[38] Rollock was also a devoted pastor, and although he could claim no parish experience, 'his students were his parishioners, and most conscientiously did he look after them'.[39] In its first principal, then, Edinburgh had someone in whom the role of pastor was combined with that of teacher, piety in the service of learning. The roles serve one another, as every good Christian teacher knows. What, though, when the choice (if it comes to that) is between erudition or scholarly distinction and those pastoral gifts which, in combination with obvious learning, in Rollock's case at least, gave his teaching its

[36] *Studies in Scottish Church History*, p. 33.
[37] *Ibid.*, p. 34.
[38] *Ibid.*, p. 35.
[39] *Ibid.*, p. 37.

memorable quality? Professor Cheyne's answer: 'Had Edinburgh's Town Council turned, for their first University Principal, not to Rollock but to Napier of Merchiston, that mathematician of genius, they might have secured an abler man. They would hardly have got a better—and even in academic appointments it may, just occasionally, be wise to take other things than intellect into consideration'.[40]

A somewhat different, but no less laudatory, picture is given of the saintly Robert Leighton, Principal of Edinburgh University from 1653 to 1662, and the second of Edinburgh's 'three exemplars' of piety and learning. A great admirer of Rollock, Leighton was if anything more interested in piety than learning, if that is the right way to put it. As principal he preached weekly on Sunday mornings in the University Church, and once or twice monthly on Sunday afternoons in the College Hall. There were also occasional lectures to students, particularly at graduation. 'But of central importance were the lectures which—reviving a custom of his hero, Rollock—he gave each Wednesday in the Common Hall on a variety of theological topics. Scarcely distinguishable from sermons, these 'prelections' ... were, essentially, exhortations to a devout and holy life ...'.[41] Although Leighton was an accomplished Latinist and widely read in both classical and patristic literature, one of the 'marks of his religion' was 'its careful subordination of scholarship—for which he professed the highest regard—to what he would

[40] *Ibid.*, p. 39.
[41] *Ibid.*, p. 42.

undoubtedly have considered the one thing needful. Speaking once with his nephew about his books, of which he was obviously proud, he remarked that 'one devout thought is worth them all'.[42]

Leighton was no narrow dogmatist, however. Indeed his lectures at Edinburgh, Professor Cheyne tells us, were part of 'a life-long campaign against dogmatic intolerance'—for what may be the best of reasons: 'our disputes ought to be managed with few words', Leighton urged, 'for naked truth is most effectual for its own defence, and when it is once well understood, its natural light dispels all the darkness of error'. Although it was said of Leighton that 'by many he was judged void of any dogmatic principles' and that 'he had too great a latitude of charity towards the papists', he was admired by as diverse a company as Philip Dodderidge, John Wesley, S. T. Coleridge, McLeod Campbell, John Tullock and Robert Flint. 'We may well concede', says Professor Cheyne, 'that his richest legacy was the example of his character and the unusual blend of piety and learning which he bequeathed to the academic world'.[43]

If in Robert Leighton the balance of piety and learning was on the side of piety, it may be said (in complete charity) that in William Carstares, the third 'exemplar', it was on the side of learning. Principal of Edinburgh University in his final years (1703–15), Carstares, like Leighton, 'could be described as a product of the Puritan tradition', but unlike Leighton, 'he did not abandon his

[42] *Ibid.*, p. 44.
[43] *Ibid.*, pp. 45–6.

father's cause, but worked and suffered for it until its triumph—modified and liberalized—at the Revolution. .Theologically trained in Utrecht, probably ordained there, and devoted to the work of the ministry, 'he seems quite early to have decided that the exceptional circumstances of the time called for political involvement …' and so while in the Netherlands entered the service of William of Orange, 'the chief hope of those opposed to Charles II and his successor James'.[44] By turns secret agent, prisoner in both the Towers of London and the Tollbooth, and the Castle at Edinburgh (for being implicated in conspiracies against Charles), minister of a dissenting congregation near London, chaplain (again in the Netherlands) to William, and (during William's reign in Britain) the monarch's chief adviser on Scottish affairs and prime mover in the establishment of Presbyterianism in Scotland, as well as a primary influence for moderation in the Kirk's General Assembly in 1690 and the important years immediately thereafter. 'Thanks in large measure to Carstares and men like him', says Professor Cheyne, 'the Church which moved forward into the eighteenth century showed some signs of that urbane reasonableness which was to be its pride in the age of William Robertson, Alexander Carlyle, and the great Evangelical leader, John Erskine'.[45]

But it is Carstares's presidency of the University during 'the momentous change from instruction by regents to instruction by specialist professors that put all

[44] *Ibid.*, p. 47.
[45] *Ibid.*, p. 50.

succeeding generations of Edinburgh students in his debt'. By the beginning of the eighteenth century the University possessed 'something very like a Faculty of Divinity in embryo', with a Chair of Divinity, Chairs of Hebrew and Oriental Languages and Ecclesiastical History (created in 1702); and in 1708, under Carstares's guidance, what would later become the arts faculty also saw 'the final abandonment of the old system in which four regents taught Greek, together with all the branches of Philosophy, each to his own cohort of students'. From then on Greek was taught by one professor and Philosophy divided among three sub-specialities. 'The age of specialist scholars had come into being at a clap', says Professor Cheyne. Edinburgh University was thus 'poised for take-off into the modern world, and there is pretty general argument among authorities that no single person was more responsible than William Carstares'.[46]

That is Carstares as regards learning. What of piety? 'Appropriately for one who is often regarded as the architect of eighteenth-century Moderatism, Carstares did not wear his heart on his sleeve', Professor Cheyne tells us. 'Though laden with honours, Principal of the University and minister in succession of Greyfriars and the High Kirk (St Giles), he was known also for his kindness to the distressed clergy of Scottish Episcopalianism and to the distressed of his own communion. The *Scots Courant* summed him up rather well when, two days after his death, it described him as "a

---

[46] *Ibid.*, pp. 51–2.

man of great worth, piety, and learning, and very charitable to the poor'".[47]

In 'John and Donald Baillie: A Biographical Introduction' we have a slightly different approach in that the Baillies, especially John, did actually comment on the question of Christian faith and academic inquiry, no less of a scientific and humane than of a theological sort. The fact, President John Mackay of Princeton Seminary observed, that we have in John Baillie's work (Donald's name should be included too, Professor Cheyne added) 'combined the finest scholarship with a deep devotional spirit harks back to Highland religion at its best';[48] but 'alongside the influence exerted by Highland theology and piety', Professor Cheyne reminds us, 'there existed in the minds of the youthful Baillies the very different, and at times frankly inimical, inheritance of humanist culture'.[49] In the reminiscences which served as the introduction to his brother's *The Theology of the Sacraments*, John recalled their days at school: 'our minds, for example, were soon set afire by the reading of Shakespeare, but there was no room at all for Shakespeare within the Puritanism of our early upbringing; no room for theatre of any kind; but no room especially for Shakespeare's large and generous and delicately discriminating appreciation of the human scene'.[50]

[47]   *Ibid.*, p. 53.
[48]   *Ibid.*, p. 202.
[49]   *Ibid.*, p. 205.
[50]   *Ibid.*, p. 206.

Professor Cheyne perceptively notes that 'There is considerable room for debate about the details—perhaps even the desirability—of the reconciliation which the Baillies later sought to effect between humanistic culture and traditional theology. What cannot be disputed, however, is that neither John nor Donald was in any doubt as to the need for such a reconciliation; and that if they eventually attained an eminent place among the Christian thinkers of their time they were also, without equivocation, men of the modern world'.[51] There were for the Baillies, in other words, important apologetic uses of learning. During their university years both laboured to come to grips with 'the most negative aspects of modern thought so far as Christian faith was concerned': faith in evolutionary progress, atheistic humanism, mechanistic materialism, and so on. 'Yet in all their struggles with the difficulties created for traditional orthodoxy by recent developments in European thought the Baillies never allowed themselves to draw a sharply divisive line between faith and culture. What they did, rather, was to counter unbelieving humanism with the weapons of the mainstream humanist tradition of the West' [52]—learning, that is, in defence of faith.

But this was no merely reactionary response. Indeed, with regard to science John said: 'It is to our Christian advantage to pursue our scientific researches with unabated vigour. No good will ever come of setting any limit to the advance of scientific knowledge'. 'At the same

[51]   *Ibid.*, p. 206–7.
[52]   *Ibid.*, pp. 207–8.

time', writes Professor Cheyne, 'he warned against an even more fatal error than "curtailing scientific enquiry to make room for faith", namely, "to allow our faith to be stifled by our science". "Neither science nor faith must be abandoned", Baillie urged, "by abating either to give the other the greater room, or by whittling down both so that they may be more easily mortised. What we must rather do is to accept this strain as inherent in our human situation, resolutely resisting the temptation to resolve it in a premature way, living with it humbly as befits us, and profiting by the discipline it imposes, until such time as a maturer wisdom brings its own better solution"'.[53]

Such wise counsel is reflective of the Baillies' profoundly apologetic concerns—piety's answer to learning—for as Professor Cheyne reminds us, 'Whatever else may be said about them, the brothers were pre-eminently apologists for the Faith ...'.[54] And foundational to John's apologetic concerns was an understanding that our knowledge of God is one of 'mediated immediacy'; that is (quoting John McIntyre, Baillie's successor in Divinity at New College), 'a rejection of the idea that we know God directly and intuitively, by means of some sixth sense, which some have and some do not have'. No, our knowledge of God occurs 'in, with, and under' other entities, 'such as other selves, the world, human history'. The university setting is therefore 'not irrelevant', says McIntyre (interpreting Baillie), 'for God is thought to be known in those fields in which other disciplines

---

[53]   *Ibid.*, p. 216.
[54]   *Ibid.*, p. 219.

operate'.[55] Learning is important—we might say essential—to piety, because our knowledge of God to a certain degree depends upon it.

There was too John Baillie's deep appreciation for both the critical role the Christian Tradition played in the history of the West—he spoke of those who rejected the Christian Tradition as 'those who lived on its dividends without declaring their capital'[56]—and the debt owed Greek intellectual culture by modern theological education. He believed that 'the modern theological school had its origin in two very diverse but confluent sources: Jesus' teaching of the twelve, and the education provided by the schools of Athens',[57] and that contrary to historians like Harnack, this was a salutary thing. Humane studies not only have their apologetic uses; they are by history bound up with divine studies, and that fact should be acknowledged.

Finally, there is the very practical matter of the role of the Christian minister. His effectiveness at fulfilling it, John wrote, can be measured 'in one way only—by his success at meeting the religious needs of the whole community'. Moreover, he said, 'In a modern community he can have no such success unless he is able, among other things, to inspire general confidence in himself as a keen-minded, fearless and well-equipped seeker of the truth about God and Man and Life and Destiny'. The job of the seminary, therefore, is to equip men for such

[55] *Ibid*, p. 220.
[56] *Ibid*., p. 220.
[57] *Ibid*., p. 222.

leadership; and that will be done by teaching them to *think*—'to think fairly, to think deeply, to think boldly, to think humbly. I think that there are no questions that should be more in our minds about the students we graduate than these: Do they clearly know exactly what they are recommending when they recommend Christianity? And do they clearly know, and profoundly feel, why it is more worthy to be recommended than any other solution to the great riddle of life?' [58] Or, as he put it elsewhere: 'Within Western civilization the priest is not likely to be effective if he is not a scholar too'.[59]

In addition to being able speakers and effective organizers, John urged, pastors must be men who 'can answer, in such a way as to inspire trust, the very often independent questionings of the modern mind'. Moreover, 'if the Church will but realize in a really enterprising way her role as teacher, she has a magnificent future before her in our generation'. Thus did John Baillie strive, concludes Professor Cheyne, 'as few of his generation did to present a clear and cogent case for Christian faith, to strengthen the ties which by tradition have bound Church and University together, and to raise the standards of theological education not only in his homeland but throughout the English-speaking world'.[60]

The relevance of all of this for the life and work of Professor Cheyne is not difficult to see. In the Baillies he

---

[58]   *Ibid.*, pp. 223–4.
[59]   *Ibid.*, p. 222.
[60]   *Ibid.*, p. 224.

found much to admire and emulate: along with their Liberal Evangelical commitment to a historical and literary approach to the Bible, their wariness of what seemed an undue emphasis on creedal and confessional statements, and their respect for the methods of natural science, there was in them both a most attractive combination of what John Mackay called the finest scholarship and a deep devotional spirit.

In his comments on Robert Rollock there is echoed much that could be said, indeed has been said, of Professor Cheyne himself: 'an especially effective *teacher*, genuinely interested in his students and ever desirous of finding the best way to communicate with them'; 'his regime seems to have been marked by a good deal of lenity and compassion'. Likewise Robert Leighton and William Carstares: dislike of dogmatic intolerance and an unusual blend of piety and learning in Leighton, the moderation and 'urbane reasonableness' of Carstares.

Of Alexander Campbell Cheyne, Professor Shaw writes: 'Although the future will remember him as a scholar, it was a teacher that he is best known by the present generation and would, I think, himself like best to be remembered'.[61] And for all of the wit and wisdom and winsomeness, the professionalism, scholarship and culture that characterized his teaching, what contributed most to his being a great teacher may be that he was simply a genuinely Christian man. It was obvious that he cared about his craft, about what and how he taught. It

[61]   *Scottish Christianity in the Modern World*, p. 10.

was just as obvious that he cared about *those* he taught. As one of his graduate students I may have enjoyed privileges undergraduates did not. I am not sure. But I have never forgotten his and Mona's generous interest in my and my family's welfare. One Christmas there was a knock at the door; when we answered there was a huge box sitting on the step, and Professor Cheyne and Mona were slipping away in her little Volkswagen. The box contained all the makings of a holiday meal, including candles and table cloth. How did they know it was a particularly lean graduate student Christmas? There were, too, the invitations to use the flat in Peebles: 'You and Florence need a rest', Professor Cheyne would simply say, and, come to think of it, we probably did. Many others have testified to a similar kindness and generosity. So, yes, scholar, teacher, friend—also Christian example. While teaching at Glasgow he had realized that he had 'a kind of pastoral view of students' and was wanting more for them than he could provide as a lecturer. That was part of his motivation in deciding for the ministry. Teaching at New College gave him the opportunity for both lecturing and ministering, and both, especially in combination, were executed nobly. 'His students were his parishioners, and most conscientiously did he look after them'.

~

18

Postscript

~

PROFESSOR Cheyne died on 31 March 2006, peacefully, in his sleep, at Hay Lodge Hospital, Peebles. He was laid to rest next to Mona (who died in 1999) on 22 April on a cold, blustery spring day in Stobo churchyard amidst daffodils everywhere at their golden best and verdant hillsides covered with sheep, and lambs newly born. This was his beloved Borders, the stunningly beautiful and peaceful Tweed River Valley, and it was all wonderfully and appropriately Scottish. Even the weather, the wind and mist and grey, spoke eloquently of Scotland and Tweeddale.

Stobo church, one of the oldest in Scotland and redolent of ages long gone—the main structure dates to the twelfth century, parts of it possibly to the sixth— could hardly have been better suited to remembrances of a minister and historian of the Kirk: shaped by both its Reformation and pre-Reformation past, it once served (following the Reformation and prior to 1633) as parish school as well as centre of worship—another reminder of Scotland's, and Professor Cheyne's, commitment both to learning and Christian piety.

The service, attended by 50 or 60 friends from both the academic and local communities, was simple and dignified: three congregational hymns ('The Saviour Died, But Rose Again', 'Where High The Heavenly Temple Stands', and 'Be Still My Soul'), a lesson from 2 Corinthians 4:16–5:1 and Psalm 23 (read in Old Scots), and two eulogies. The music that carried the congregation forth was 'Requiescat in Pace' by Dr George Cheyne, Professor Cheyne's brother, who died only three months earlier.

The eulogists were Professor Stewart J. Brown, Professor Cheyne's successor in the Chair at New College, and the Reverend Jack Kellet, long-time friend of, and pastor to, the Cheyne family.

Professor Brown spoke of Professor Cheyne's 'quiet dignity, his commitment to the life of learning, his gracious manner, and his gentle sense of humour'. He was 'an old-style Scottish Professor, with sturdy independence of mind', Professor Brown recalled. But, 'I never met with him—whether as a student, or later as a friend—that I didn't come away feeling that I had been somehow helped to be a better person, that I had been given guidance, not only in scholarship, but how to live a more caring and fulfilling life'.

Professor Brown also dwelt on Professor Cheyne's greatness as a teacher—'his lectures were almost legendary'—and his wide-ranging erudition, remarking, perceptively, that Professor Cheyne 'was a scholar, rather than a researcher; he was a man of letters in the old sense'.

He also mentioned Professor Cheyne's leadership as head of the department of Ecclesiastical History in New College, 'the famed "Cheyne gang" of David Wright in early Church History, Peter Matheson in Reformation history, and Andrew Ross in the history of Christian missions and American Church history', ably assisted by May Hocking, 'a superb administrative secretary'. This department of Ecclesiastical History was 'probably the best in the United Kingdom in talent and breadth of coverage', he said. Moreover, Professor Cheyne's tenure was part of 'a great era for New College—a time of inspired academic leadership in the various disciplines, a time when New College's international reputation soared, …'.

The Reverend Kellet's homily was titled 'Alec Cheyne: Friend and Fellow Disciple' and his theme, 'Blessed are the Meek'. 'Oh, Alec', he said, 'How truly blest are the meek'. 'To be meek is to be very strong indeed'. 'Alec captivated his students: he did not seek to capture us'— and returning to a subject remarked on by almost everyone: 'Alec—the best teacher we ever had—seemed always to hold *us* in high regard. *Together* we were engaged in the Lord's service: and he was interested in us and our doings elsewhere, as well as our learning in class'.

Of Professor Cheyne's life-long commitment to the Christian ministry, Reverend Kellet said: 'Alec, unlike so many in recent years, never lost the convictions that Scotland flourishes by the preaching of the Word, and that the parish ministry was the most important job one could commit oneself to in life'. He went on to reveal what he reckoned was not generally known in academic circles, namely, that 'Alec involved himself in inquiries about an Aberdeen parish vacancy some years after he'd achieved 'the plateau and prestige' of his Edinburgh chair'. It was the combination in Professor Cheyne of erudition and life-long commitment to Christian service that Reverend Kellet underscored; also that winsome blend in him of academic distinction and evident humility.

There were amusing and charming anecdotes as well. Of the decidedly un-domestic bachelor Alec, for instance, once asked by his hostess at dinner to slice a loaf of bread. Alec was enthralled, Reverend Kellet remembered: 'This is great fun', Alec said; 'I've never done it before'. In a similar case of domestic impracticality, he once had to call in an electrician after failing to get a light bulb to remain in its socket!

In his closing prayer of thanksgiving and intercession Reverend Kellet offered 'our solemn and hearty thanks for the good life of our teacher ... colleague ... writer ... *non-pareil*—for our strong and very human friend, Alexander Campbell Cheyne'.

Amen, and Amen.

BIBLIOGRAPHY

BOOKS

The Transforming of the Kirk: Victorian Scotland's Religious Revolution (Edinburgh: The Saint Andrew Press, 1983).

Studies in Scottish Church History (Edinburgh: T&T Clark, 1999). Most of the essays included in this volume were first published elsewhere. They are listed separately below (distinguished by *) because, as noted in the Acknowledgements (p. v above), 'in some instances considerable changes have subsequently been made in them'.

Practical and the pious: essays on Thomas Chalmers (1780–1847), Editor (Edinburgh: Saint Andrew Press, 1985).

Scottish Piety over Five Centuries – A Miscellany, forthcoming (Edinburgh: Dunedin Press, 2007) ISBN 978-1-903765-78-4.

ESSAYS

'Inter-Church Relations: A Retrospect', *Scottish Journal of Theology*, xii (1959), 275–76.

'The Westminster Standards: A Century of Re-Appraisal', *Records of the Scottish Church History Society*, xiv (1963), 199–214.

'Diversity and Development in Scottish Presbyterianism', *New College Bulletin*, ii:1 (1965), 7–20.*

'Worship in the Kirk: Knox, Westminster, and the 1940 Book' in Duncan Shaw (ed.), *Reformation and Revolution* (Edinburgh, The Saint Andrew Press, 1967), 70–81.

'Introduction' to John Tulloch, *Movements of Religious Thought in Britain During the Nineteenth Century* (Leicester: Leicester University Press, 1971). This is a reprint of Tulloch's original of the same title of 1885.

'Turning Points in Scottish Church History', a series in *Life and Work*, January to December, 1978 (except for October, when no instalment appeared), plus the final instalment of February 1979.

'The Place of the Confession Through Three Centuries' in Alasdair I. C. Heron (ed.), *The Westminster Confession in the Church Today* (Edinburgh: The Saint Andrew Press 1982), 17–27.

'Piety and Learning: Three Edinburgh Exemplars', *New College Bulletin* (1983), 2–9.*

'The Bible and Change in the Nineteenth Century' in David F. Wright (ed.), *The Bible in Scottish Life and Literature* (Edinburgh: The Saint Andrew Press 1988), 192–207.*

'Church Reform and Church Defence: The Contribution of John Tulloch', *Records of the Scottish Church History Society*, xxiii (1989), 397–416.*

'The Baillies and Scottish Theology: their inheritance and their legacy' in D. W. D. Shaw (ed.) *In divers manners: a St Mary's miscellany* (St Andrews, 1990), 84–144.

'John Caird: Preacher, Professor, Principal' in W. I. P. Hazlett (ed.), *Traditions of Theology in Glasgow, 1450-1990* (Edinburgh: Scottish Academic Press, 1993), 43–58.*

'The Baillie brothers: a biographical introduction' and 'The Baillies' churchmanship' in D. Fergusson (ed.), *Christ, Church and Society: Essays on John Baillie and Donald Baillie* (Edinburgh: T & T Clark 1993), 3–37 and 173–198.*

The Ten Years' Conflict and The Disruption: An Overview (Edinburgh: Scottish Academic Press 1993). This is a booklet of 17 pages.*

'Thoughts on Confessional Subscription', *Theology in Scotland*, ii:1 (1995), 5–16.

'Bible and Confession in Scotland: The Background to the Robertson Smith Case' in William Johnstone (ed.), *William Robertson Smith: Essays in Reassessment* (Sheffield: Sheffield Academic Press 1995), 24–40.

'New College, Edinburgh 1846-1996: The Spirit of New College'. a pamphlet (20 pages) published for the 150th anniversary of New College in 1996.*

'Ecclesiastical History' in D. F. Wright and G. D. Badcock (eds.), *Disruption to Diversity: Edinburgh Divinity, 1846–1996* (Edinburgh: T&T Clark 1996), 99–116.*

'The Religious World of Henry Drummond', *Theology in Scotland*, v (1999), 5–20.*

The Ten Years' Conflict and The Disruption: An Overview (rev. edn.) (Edinburgh: Dunedin Academic Press, 2005). This is a booklet (18 pages), a revision of the one published in 1993 (Edinburgh: Scottish Academic Press). The essay also appears in *Studies in Scottish Church History.*

REVIEWS

Gordon Donaldson, *The Scottish Reformation* (1960), in *Scottish Journal of Theology*, xvi (1963), 78–88.

A. L. Drummond and J. Bulloch, *The Church in Late Victorian Scotland, 1874–1900* (1978) in *Scottish Journal of Theology*, xxxii (1979), 487–91.

WORKS IN PROFESSOR CHEYNE'S HONOUR

S. J. Brown and G. Newlands (eds.), *Scottish Christianity in the Modern World* (Edinburgh: T&T Clark, 2000).

David F. Wright, 'From a Quarter so totally Unexpected: Translation of the Early Church Fathers in Victorian Scotland', *Records of the Scottish Church History Society*, xxx (2000), 124–169.

INDEX